Abundant Life

Realizing the promises of Jesus

Alison C. Ludwig

Contents

I write to discover what I think.

-- Daniel Boorstin

The best things can't be told; the second
best are misunderstood.

-- Heinrich Zimmer

Introduction

The Bible – the unquestioned Word of God for millions of Americans and guide to living for millions more around the world. Ninety-six percent of Americans believe in God, but only 19 percent regularly practice their religion. Forty-five percent of religious Americans are more likely to follow their own instincts than denominational teachings.[1] Could those "instincts" be the still, small voice of God? There is a huge number of Americans who are seeking spiritual fulfillment, but aren't finding it in mainstream churches. Most churches subscribe to a creed, and to be a member of that church you must believe, or agree to pretend to believe, the statements in that creed. The Bible has been the subject of much scholarly research for the past 30 years. We now know something about the Bible's human authors, when the books were written, and how they were selected for inclusion.

Many people consider themselves good Christians because they have asked Jesus to forgive their sins and they regularly attend and actively participate in church. I had been a Christian for 34 years. Not a Christian as in when someone asks what church you go to, and you say Methodist. Christian as in, I had lived every day of my life for the previous 18 years the best that I could for God, going to church every week, singing in the choir, teaching Sunday school. I talked to God. I felt I had a relationship with Him and that He had personally guided me to the place I was in life. I had always thought of the Gospels as eyewitness accounts of Jesus' life. That was one of the reasons I had become a Christian – because of what I believed Jesus had said.

Then I participated in an in-depth Bible study, and along with all the wonderful things I learned, I also learned that the gospels had been written decades after Jesus was crucified, and at least two of them were written by people who had witnessed none of it. It is estimated that the book of Mark was written about 30 years after Jesus was crucified. Matthew's and Luke's gospels were written about 15 years after that, and the book of John was written about 15 years after those. There is some disagreement about exactly when they were written, but most scholars do not argue about the order of them and none argue that they were written immediately after Jesus' death or earlier. Some people believe in divine dictation of the Bible. Most people believe that the Bible is accurate, but for me the passage of 30 to 60 years puts some doubt on the exact quotes of Jesus, and makes likely that things could have been added to the historical facts in light of the authors' and editors subsequent influences.

The second thing I noticed is that what Paul preached in the letters that make up half of the books of the New Testament was not the same as what Jesus preached in the gospels. Jesus preached repentance; his focus was on encouraging people to do God's will, to let go of the traditions of men and return to the commands of God. He didn't come to replace the Jewish law, but to fulfill it. His mission: to get people to remove the things that were separating them from God so they could enact the kingdom of God on earth. Paul preached the gospel of grace and the *gift* of righteousness. All he required was that people believe what he said, that Jesus was the Son of God, the Christ of Hebrew scripture. He preached that everyone who believes is forgiven for everything they could not escape from under the law. His mission: to convert people to belief in a divine sacrifice.

The books we now know as the New Testament represent only a fraction of the writings of the Christian communities of the first three centuries AD. As many as 50 gospels were in circulation at that time. In 327 AD, the Christian scholar Eusebius selected 26 of the current 27 books of the New Testament plus a couple of others as recognized by every orthodox author he knew or recognized by some and disputed by others. In 350 AD, Cyril, Bishop of Jerusalem removed the Epistle of Barnabus, the book of Hermas, and possibly others from the list produced by Eusebius. St. Athanasius, bishop of Alexandria, added the book of Revelation, establishing our current list in 367 A.D.[2] Which books were to be considered Holy Scripture and which were not, was decided by the fourth century church, not by God, Jesus, or the Apostles. Paul's letters were included in the New Testament because they had been accepted by the fourth century orthodox church.

Even as a faithful Christian there were some concepts I had trouble understanding or believing. The first was the virgin birth and the whole concept of a son of God, which seemed polytheistic to me. With a 20th century understanding of reproduction, I had trouble believing that God physically impregnated Mary. I believed that Joseph was the physical father and not just the stepfather of Jesus.

With my 20th century understanding of death, I wondered if either Jesus was not really dead when he was buried or if he never rose from the tomb. I also had trouble understanding exactly what Christ's sacrifice was if he did rise from the dead. Being mocked? Being scourged? Being separated from God for three days? Does that sound like adequate compensation for all the sins that would ever be committed by millions of people? And I had trouble with the whole concept that one man's sacrifice could somehow make up for the sins of millions of other people. But atoning sacrifice was never emphasized in the churches I belonged to, so I accepted these mysteries of the faith.

Another thing I noticed during the in-depth Bible study was that the story of the virgin birth (or any birth for that matter) is only included in the books of Matthew and Luke. These same gospels include genealogies tracing the lineage of Jesus from Abraham through David and *Joseph*. Mark and John do not include genealogies or birth stories. Also, throughout his ministry, Jesus was essentially homeless and hounded by people begging for healing. The sacrifice that he made was during his short ministry.

Many may find my writing heretical, for "All Scripture is God-breathed and is useful for teaching..." Let's see, who wrote that? Oh, yes, it was Paul. How convenient of him to testify to the truth of his own testimony. It saves the trouble of establishing truth by the testimony of two or three witnesses. Josh McDowell, in his book *Evidence that Demands a Verdict*, first establishes the authority of the Bible as a whole as a historical document. He makes no distinction between the Old Testament and the New Testament, no distinction between narrative accounts and evangelistic letters. He relies on Old Testament books such as Chronicles to establish the authority of books such as John and Romans. He uses the words of Paul's letters and the later books of the New Testament to "prove" Paul's message that Jesus is the Christ is true. The Bible is not one book by one author. It is a collection of writings.

The 20th century German Christian "[Karl Ludwig] Schmidt insisted that the Christian understanding of Jesus Christ was not negotiable... the opposition between Christians and Jews was reaffirmed by Schmidt as essential to Christianity... 'We Christians must never tire of keeping this one conflict alive.'" On the other side of the Atlantic during the 20th century, the Moody Bible Institute was publishing the "Fundamentals" of Christianity: (1) The literal inerrancy of the Bible (2) the virgin birth of Jesus (3) the sacrificial death of Christ (4) the resurrection of Christ (5) and the imminent return of Christ.[3] "Christianity understands itself as the absolute religion, intended for all men, which cannot recognize any other religion besides itself as of equal right."[4] This stance of digging heels in for a fight instead of engaging in reasonable dialogue left Christianity out of the 20th century process of uncovering and correcting entrenched fallacies of belief that other disciplines, such as the physical and social sciences underwent. It also misplaced the emphasis of Christianity on "correct" beliefs rather than right actions.

One summer I read *The Golden Bough* by James Frazer, a history of ancient magic and religion. This book touched off a crisis in my spiritual life. It was critical in dislodging Christian beliefs that I had held for years, so I include here brief paraphrases from that book. "Son of a god" was a common concept in religions of the Syrian region. Some men and women were considered to be the sons and daughters of a god, supposed to have literally been conceived by god's holy spirit in the wombs of mortal women. The death and resurrection of a god, another concept troubling to minds at the dawn of the 21st century, was extremely common in ancient religions, applying to Adonis in Western Asia and the Greek empire, Attis, Tammuz in Sumeria and Phoenicia, and Dionysus in Crete.

The concept of vicarious sacrifice is also ancient. In ancient Thessaly, kings were sacrificed as representatives of their people until they managed to shift the fatal burden to their sons. The Negroes of West Africa laid their hands on a human victim to transfer their sin to him, took off his head, and offered his blood to the gods to appease divine wrath. The Brahmas transferred the sins of their people into one or more cows; then the sins were carried away with the cows. Periodically, the Albanians of Eastern Caucasus would sacrifice a sacred slave by piercing his heart with a spear.

Then all the people stood on the body as a ceremony to transfer their sins to the victim.

In New Zealand a fern stalk was tied to a man and all the sins of the people were transferred to him. He then jumped into the river and untied the stalk, allowing it to float away to the sea, carrying their sins with it. When the Bagunda army returned from war with evil attached to the soldiers, it was customary to transfer the evil to a female slave and three animals. The slave and animals were sent back to the country from which they had come, their limbs were broken, and they and the evil were left to die.

The transference of sin to an animal also has ancient Hebrew roots. On the Day of Atonement, the Jewish high priest laid both his hands on the head of a live goat, confessed over it all the sins of the Israelites, transferring the sins of the people to the goat, and sent it away into the wilderness, the original scapegoat. In the first century A.D. vicarious sacrifice was not a new concept and it was not a strange concept.

The sacrament of Holy Communion also has ancient Pagan roots. At Aricia loaves baked in human form were eaten sacramentally by worshippers of a divine spirit. In Sweden, a loaf which represents the corn spirit is baked in the shape of a little girl. This loaf is divided and eaten to ingest the corn spirit itself. The Aztecs also practiced the custom of breaking a bread image of a god in pieces and eating it sacramentally as the body of a god. The ancient Mexicans believed the theological doctrine of bread becoming body. All who ate the consecrated bread entered into a mystic communion with their god by receiving a portion of the bread.[5]

Innocence Shattered

Could it be just coincidence that so many of the basic tenets of Christianity were common in the religions which preceded it? Was my entire life built on an ancient myth? Unable to continue to participate in church life while questioning its basic beliefs and unwilling to just walk away from church, I began an intensive search for truth. I read many books by religious scholars and I delved even deeper into the Bible. What I found caused me to make some changes in how I lived and changed my perspective on church. When the books of the New Testament are read in chronological order, a very clear evolution emerges from the teaching of Jesus to the theology of Paul. My studies led me to the conclusion that God is real. Jesus lived and preached and healed. And I assembled a hypothesis about Paul and about Christianity. This book contains some of my opinions, but most of what it contains is truths unearthed from the Bible and the writings of religious scholars. But the purpose of this book is not to question theological doctrine. It is to lead people to the very real spiritual fulfillment that they seek.

Paul, considered the author of half of the books of the New Testament, was an educated Roman citizen who lived among the pagans of Cyprus, Macedonia, Syria, and Galatia for 12 years before writing most of his letters. Adding this to the new information about ancient religions, I assembled a hypothesis: Paul injected elements which appealed to the Mediterranean mind into the message of Jesus, enabling it to spread quickly among people ready to abandon their ancient idol worship, but still clinging to some of its trappings. The Roman execution of Jesus contributed more than anything else to spread his doctrines throughout the Roman Empire. It added on to what had previously been an ethical mission the framework of a divine revelation culminating in the passion and death of the incarnate son of a heavenly father. In this form, the story of the life and death of Jesus carried an influence which it could never have had if he had died a natural death.

In *The Raft is Not the Shore*, author Nhat Hanh said that what someone sees "depends not only on the thing you exhibit but on the nature and the substance of the one who looks." He is speaking specifically about Jesus. What people saw in Jesus depended not only on who and what Jesus was, but also on who and what they were. Paul never saw the living Jesus. He knew of his followers. He knew the Jewish traditions. He came to know the traditions of the pagans he lived and traveled among. The Christ which Paul spread as a missionary and in his letters depended on who Paul was and who he became.

For centuries between the consolidation of the church in the 4th century and the invention of the printing press in the 1500 AD, the Roman Catholic Church held a monopoly on the dissemination of religious information. Only the very rich could afford books and only the very educated could read them. The church did not hold public Bible readings or Bible studies.   They selected and emphasized what they chose. When printed Bibles became widely available, the monopoly was broken, and as people began to read the Bible, they began to break away from the Catholic Church. The most successful of these began the Protestant reform movement.   The more radical were burned at the stake by the still enormously powerful Catholic Church.   In his novel *Joshua, The Homecoming*, Joseph Girzone wrote that it is when religion becomes a cult that it forbids freedom of discussion. Through the centuries, Christian leaders have used "intimidation and brute force in an attempt to gain the control that they could not win by honest and reasonable discussion of issues…The Book did not just drop down out of heaven. Who said we have to accept it for our salvation? People cannot just decide that and then impose it on the whole world." Eminent Scottish professor William Robertson Smith "maintained that the Bible was the word of God, but that the word was held inside a record made by many men over a considerable period of time, and that, as with all of man's enterprises, errors and imperfections were inevitable, and therefore careful analysis of the text was not only desirable but essential."[6]

The early Church is often spoken of as if it were one monolithic institution. In reality, the Church grew in different ways and as the result of various forces. As the early Church took root in different areas, local beliefs, mythologies, and practices were incorporated. Gradually, versions of the Christ story that had common elements came together and were defined into standard Christian teaching, and those that were too radical or heretical were banished or resisted. The ideal of One Church is a historical invention of the fourth and fifth centuries.[7] In the book *A Place at the Table*, Matthew Fox points out that Jesus was not present at the Council of Nicea in 325 AD which is when the Catholic church created so much of what we know of as Christianity.

There were three Christian movements during the first few decades after Jesus' ministry. The first was a Jewish Christian movement led by James and Jesus' disciples. The second was Pauline Christianity. The third was Gnostic Christianity which combined Jewish teachings with Asian and Babylonian teachings. Each of these had very different views of Jesus. In the Roman retaliation for the Bar Kochba Jewish revolt in 132-135 AD, all Jews, including Jewish Christians were killed, enslaved, or permanently driven from Palestine. That left two Christian movements. The Gnostics died out about a hundred years later. That left Pauline Christianity.[8] The aim of this book is to resurrect a form of Christianity which is truer to Jesus' original mission, bringing with it the blessings which he promised. Walk with me now through the earliest books of the New Testament.

Part One:
Jesus vs. Paul: The Search for Truth

James – Faith without deeds is useless

With my theory that Paul transformed the teaching and mission of Jesus during his years living among pagans, I looked to the oldest books of the New Testament in my search for truth. The oldest book included in the New Testament is the book of James written by Jesus' brother. It is a beautiful book continuing the teachings of Jesus. James says not to deceive yourselves by just listening to God's word; *do* what it says. The one who continues to study the Hebrew scriptures, and does not forget what he has heard, but does it—he will be blessed.[a]

Jesus and his brother James were focused on doing the will of God. James asked what good it was if a man claimed to have faith but did nothing about it. He questioned whether such faith could save a person. If someone doesn't have enough clothes and food each day, saying to him, "Go, I wish you well; keep warm and well fed", does no good.[b] James also focused on the words that we speak. He wrote that we should speak and act as if we are going to be judged, because anyone who has not been merciful will be judged without mercy.[c] He

---

[a] verse 1:22
[b] 2:14
[c] verse 2:13

also wrote that we should be quick to listen, slow to speak and slow to get angry, because anger doesn't lead us to the good life that God desires.[a] We should humble ourselves as servants of God. The sick should have the elders of the church pray over them because the prayer offered in faith will make the sick person well. Ten to fifteen years after Jesus was crucified, James preached a message of action, not belief. He does include references to Jesus *Christ*, the devil, and the Lord's coming. I will address those topics in later chapters.

Paul's Letters to the Thessalonians

The next oldest books of the New Testament are Paul's two letters to the Thessalonians. They were written by the recently converted Paul after he had spent only about five years abroad, and hadn't yet ventured as far as Macedonia. He wrote them soon after the apostle Barnabus presented him to the other apostles who welcomed him. They are very much letters, doing little preaching. What preaching they do sounds very much like what Jesus and James preached. In them he writes about the Thessalonians faith in God and how they "turned to God from idols to serve the … true God" He writes how they (Paul, Silas, and Timothy) treated them "as a father deals with his own children, encouraging, comforting and urging you to live lives worthy of God… May he strengthen your hearts so

[a] 1:19

13

that you will be blameless and holy in the presence of our God and Father."

Paul wrote that we should live in order to please God, because God didn't call us to be impure, but to live a holy life. His writings tell us to avoid every kind of evil and ask that God will make you holy. He wrote that God's judgment is right, and therefore you will be counted worthy of the kingdom of God. The focus is very much on God and right living, as it was for Jesus and James. This is the gospel of Jesus. There is no focus on Jesus, no focus on beliefs about Jesus. He wrote that those who do not know God and do not obey the gospel will be punished. He does write about the coming of the Lord, after the man of lawlessness is revealed. There is only a vague reference to Jesus who rescues us from the coming wrath. I don't believe that at this point Paul had developed the concept of grace through faith in the sacrifice of Christ.

Mark – The Lord is one

By the time Paul wrote his next letter included in the New Testament he had lived among pagans for 12 years, so in my search for truth I turned to the next oldest book by a different author which is Mark's gospel. Mark is said to have been a relative of Barnabus, an early apostle. His mother's house was a meeting place for early Christians. His sources were early Christian writings and the oral tradition with which he was surrounded. Mark starts his telling of the story of Jesus with the ministry of John the Baptist followed immediately by the baptism of Jesus at age 30. Clearly to Mark there was nothing significant about Jesus' birth, childhood, or young adulthood. What was significant was his ministry and his miracles. In Mark's gospel, Jesus proclaimed the good news of God, that the kingdom of God is imminent. He called on people to repent of their sins. The emphasis was not on forgiveness but on change. He came to turn sinners to God's will. After he had preached and healed many people in Capernum he said, "Let us go…to the nearby villages so I can preach there also. That is why I have come." I have come to preach, to teach people how they should live. He sent out the twelve disciples to preach repentance.

When asked which is the most important commandment, Jesus responded: "the Lord our God, the Lord is one. Love the Lord your God with all your heart and with all your soul and with all your mind and with all your strength." Asked to pick out the most important sentences from the Jewish books of law, Jesus picked out "the Lord our God, the Lord is one." Not two. Not three. The Lord is one. Love him with all your heart, soul, mind, and strength.

The Lord's Supper has been interpreted by the church as Jesus' new covenant, voluntarily offering his body and blood as atonement for sins. This first gospel account of the meal does not include the words "for the forgiveness of sins" that Matthew adds about the wine, and only Luke includes "given for you" of the bread. With the help of Neil Douglas-Klotz, I offer this alternative interpretation of this last meal. Douglas-Klotz is a scholar of Aramaic, the language that Jesus spoke. Words in Aramaic do not have simple word for word translations into English; rather a single Aramaic word conveys multiple meanings. Thus the word for bread conveys not only the meaning bread, but also insight, understanding, assistance, knowledge. The word for blood also means wine, essence, consciousness.[9] So at his last supper with his disciples, Jesus took bread, gave thanks and broke it, and gave it to his disciples, saying, "Take it; this is my insight, my understanding, my knowledge." Then he took the cup, gave thanks and offered it to them, and they all drank from it. "This is my essence, which is poured out for many." This had nothing to do with the sin offerings of the Old Testament or Pagan communion rituals. This had to do with turning over all of the insight, understanding, knowledge, his very essence that he had developed over his lifetime, to his most trusted followers. It was his passing of the torch so that his work would be carried on.

In the book of Mark, Jesus answers the question of the high priest "Are you the Christ?" with "I am."[a] In the excellent book *The Four Witnesses*, Robin Griffith-Jones suggests that when Jesus was killed, his disciples were still struggling to understand who Jesus was. This lone profession attributed to Jesus could have been added by followers struggling to come to terms with who Jesus was. I shall further explore this in later chapters.

---

[a] chapter 14:62

Fairly early in his ministry, there was an incident where Jesus told unclean spirits to come out of a man and allowed them to enter a herd of pigs that then rushed into the lake and drown. This economic loss created enemies who pleaded with Jesus to leave the region. The people of his hometown took offense at him because they knew his training was as a carpenter, not a rabbi, and they knew his family. Jesus called the Pharisees hypocrites because their hearts were far from God. He said that nothing a person eats can make him unclean as the Pharisees believed; he said sexual immorality, theft, murder, adultery, envy, slander, and other sins are what make a person unclean.

Jesus was executed because he had made enemies both among leading Jews and common people. The earliest and most reliable manuscripts of the book of Mark end with verse 16:8, the empty tomb, bewilderment, fear. The story of the resurrection was added later. Mark could not possibly have originally omitted this story because he didn't think it was important. It must have been added later by followers trying to make sense of the death of their master. So in the book of Mark, Jesus was a preacher and exorcist devoted to God and advocating repentance from sin.

Matthew – Not to abolish the law but to fulfill it

The Gospel according to Matthew was written shortly after Mark. The gospel itself was not signed or the author's name mentioned within its text. It is attributed to Matthew by tradition. Matthew was one of Jesus' disciples, and as such would have been an eyewitness to most of the preaching and events recorded in his gospel. Only his accounts of Jesus' birth, childhood, baptism, and temptation would have had to have come from some indirect source. One of Matthew's main purposes in writing his account was to tie the life of Jesus to his Jewish heritage and prophecies. Matthew's genealogy traces Joseph's lineage through the kingly line, through David's son Solomon and a bunch of good and evil kings of Judah (to fulfill the prophecy of the messiah being a son of David). He somehow gets from Josiah in 609 BC to Joseph in just 13 generations (a father's average age at the birth of the child of 47 – highly unlikely. There are probably generations missing). His short and rather contrived account of the birth in Bethlehem (to fulfill the prophecy of the messiah coming from Bethlehem) includes:

- an angel appearing to Joseph in a dream telling him that Mary was pregnant by the Holy Spirit (to fulfill the prophecy of the virgin birth),
- prophesies that Jesus would save his people from their sins,
- magi following a star to a house and bringing three gifts,

- Joseph and his family fleeing to Egypt (to fulfill the prophecy of the calling of God's son out of Egypt)
- because Herod was killing male children (to fulfill the prophecy of a massacre)
- before returning to Nazareth (to fulfill the prophecy of him being called a Nazarene).

It reads as if constructed from prophecies of a messiah, rather than from interviews of Mary or anyone present. When we get to Luke we will compare this to his account.

Moving beyond the account of his birth, Matthew's Jesus said those who desire righteousness are blessed, for they will be filled. He said, "You are the salt of the earth." But if you don't serve the purpose for which you were put here, you will be thrown out and trampled. "Let your light shine before men, that they may see your good deeds and praise your Father in heaven." Matthew's Jesus preached not only against murder but also against anger, not only against adultery but also lust. He said that anyone who remarries after divorce commits adultery, going back to the original Old Testament exhortation that marriage is for life. He preached against sexual immorality, stealing, and slander.

Jesus preached against swearing oaths, advocating instead an honest and simple yes or no. He said we should not seek retribution, but instead should cooperate with adversaries. He preached loving not only your friends but also your enemies. Matthew quotes Jesus as saying "Be perfect ... as your heavenly Father is perfect."[a] Jesus said we should give to the needy anonymously, we should pray briefly and in private, and fast for God and not for appearances. He said you can't serve both God and money, and don't worry about what you will eat and drink; or about what you will wear. Jesus preached living an ethical ideal, a simple life focussed on doing God's will. He said not everyone who calls him Lord will enter the kingdom of heaven, but only he who does what his Father wants. Jesus preached a message of action, not belief. He said, "If your hand or your foot causes you to sin, cut it off and throw it away. It is better for you to enter life maimed or crippled than to have two hands or two feet and be thrown into eternal fire." There was no compromise, no shortcut. He quotes Hosea saying, "I desire mercy, and not sacrifice." He quotes God as saying, "I don't want sacrifice." Not animal sacrifice and certainly not the sacrifice of a son.

In Matthew's gospel, Jesus said that if you forgive men when they sin against you, God will also forgive you. But if you do not forgive others, your Father will not forgive your sins. He illustrated this with the parable of the Unmerciful Servant[b]. The servants in the parable are the people of the world; the king represents God. The debts are the debt that we owe God. God gives us life, talents, situations, the earth with all its bounty and beauty. In response we are supposed to "pay back" God by showing kindness and compassion to the earth

---

[a] verse 5:48
[b] chapter 18:23

and all of its inhabitants. Someone who misses those opportunities owes God a great debt. If he begs forgiveness, God takes pity on him and forgives the debt, but if that person afterwards mistreats his fellow men, showing them no compassion, God retracts his forgiveness. Jesus' God does not hand out free forgiveness. He expects mercy in action.

In Matthew, Jesus was arrested and executed because the religious leaders were offended that he didn't keep the Sabbath and follow their traditions. He was directly challenging their authority and people were following him. He was a threat to the jobs and status of the religious hierarchy, the industry of providing birds and animals for sacrifice, and a threat to the political hierarchy. Jews feared he would cause the Romans to destroy them. The Romans allowed the Jews considerable latitude in the exercise of their religion and their local government. A troublemaker threatened that freedom. A troublemaker could mean a military crackdown and the loss of their freedom to worship. He threatened life as the leading Jews of Israel knew it. Of the resurrection, Matthew writes that all eleven disciples (Judas had committed suicide) went to meet Jesus, but some doubted. The account is brief, hesitant, as if the author doesn't want to perjure himself. The post-resurrection Jesus said, "Go and make disciples of all nations, baptizing them…and *teaching them to obey* everything I have commanded you."

Luke – Repent or perish

Luke wrote his gospel at about the same time as Matthew was writing his. Luke was a gentile who had been converted by Paul. He was from Troas in Galatia. He was not an eyewitness to any of the events or dialogues. In his first few verses, he explains that he was writing an orderly account of the things he had investigated. We don't know the method or sources of his investigation. So how much of it is true? I believe that Luke did carefully investigate the life of Jesus, and most of his book is accurate. The most questionable piece is his account of the virgin birth in Bethlehem. In the book *A Place at the Table*, historian E.P. Sanders writes, "Luke... was almost certainly from Asia Minor. He...was writing his books sometime after 70 [AD], probably sometime after 80. Now in the '60s there had been great destruction because of an enormous war, the first great Jewish revolt against Rome in Palestine. This culminated with the temple's destruction in 70 AD; all the records were destroyed. People had died. Survivors had been sold into slavery. There is no newspaper archive, no encyclopedias...if he went to Palestine, he couldn't find anyone who knew anything about this... Luke uses the census of Cyrenius in his birth story and that was in 6 AD. Both Matthew and Luke place Jesus' birth during Herod's reign. Herod died in 4 BC."[10] If Jesus was born by 4 BC during Herod's reign, he couldn't have been born in Bethlehem because of the census in 6 AD.

Luke's account includes:

- An angel appearing to Mary telling her that Holy Spirit would impregnate her
- That Jesus would be the son of God and reign on the throne of his father David
- Mary's relative Elizabeth calling Mary "the mother of my lord"
- Mary's song of praise to God
- Caesar Augustus ordering a census sending Joseph (Mary's fiancé) from Nazareth to Bethlehem
- The baby Jesus being placed in a manger because there was no room at the inn
- An angel appearing to shepherds saying that the savior had been born
- A great company of the heavenly host praising God
- Joseph taking Jesus to Jerusalem where Simeon prophesized that Jesus would be a light for revelation to the gentiles, destined to cause the falling and rising of many in Israel and a sword would pierce Mary's soul
- The prophetess Anna spoke about the child to those looking forward to the redemption of Jerusalem
- The family returned to Nazareth.

This long and supernatural story confirms none of the details provided in Matthew's account but introduces many more that are not mentioned anywhere else. Luke continues to provide a genealogy tracing Joseph's lineage through David's son Nathan and an appropriate number of obscure Hebrews, not kings. Matthew and Luke don't even agree on who Joseph's father was. The only ancestor that could be the same between the two lists is Zerubbabel who would have lived around 475 BC. The only elements in common between Matthew's whole account and Luke's is that an angel (either in a dream or in person, either to Joseph or to Mary) said that the unmarried Mary (either recently had or soon would) become pregnant by the Holy Spirit. Jesus was born in Bethlehem (absolutely no details from Matthew) and (from either Egypt or Jerusalem) they went to live in Nazareth. Luke's is the kind of account you would expect to collect about the birth of someone who was later declared to be the son of God, but about which no factual details were available.

Luke was a Greek writing to Greeks. Alexander the Great was believed to be the son of Zeus. All the Macedonians regarded themselves as sons of god and that the originator of the race had actually been a god. Throughout Greek mythology, the Greek gods had intercourse with humans and begot heroic offspring. In a Greek readership, it puts Jesus in the line of the mighty heroes; it isn't a very Jewish story. It is perfectly at home in the Greek-speaking world where Christians had begun to win converts.[11] For a 21st century American readership, the appropriate response is a knowing smile and continuing on to the substance of the book.

Luke's Jesus taught that we should show love for enemies and not judge others, reinforcing Matthew's account. He taught that a man's heart is made known by his words, as did James. He asked why people called him Lord, but didn't do what he said. People who hear his words and don't put them into practice are like a man who built a house on the

24

ground without a foundation. The moment a torrent struck the house, it collapsed and was completely destroyed. It's not enough to call on the name of the Lord. Jesus preached a way of life. "My mother and brothers are those who hear God's word *and put it into practice.*" He sent out the twelve disciples to drive out unclean spirits, to cure diseases, to preach the kingdom of God and to heal the sick. With the parable of the good Samaritan, he told us how to love our neighbors. He told us we should take the time, the effort, the risk, and the expense to help anyone in need. He warned us of the consequences of materially preparing for our future but neglecting our relationship with God. He warned that if we don't bear fruit we will be cut down.

Jesus tells a story of a rich man and Lazarus. In it, the rich man requests that Lazarus warn his brothers of their impending punishment. Jesus has Abraham reply, "They have Moses and the prophets; let them listen to them….If they do not listen to Moses and the prophets, they will not be convinced [of the need to live a right life] even if someone rises from the dead." Jesus preached that people needed to follow the laws of Moses and the warnings of the prophets. He said someone rising from the dead wouldn't make any difference in who would follow God's way.

The Kingdom of God

One of Jesus' favorite topics was the kingdom of God, both while he was alive and according to Luke, during the days after his crucifixion. To most Christians this is a vague, feel-good phrase possibly referring to heaven. I propose it meant something much more concrete to Jesus and his first century followers. For 350 years before kings ruled Israel, it was governed as a theocracy, disputes resolved by judges, but the country effectively ruled by the law of God. When the Israelites saw their neighbors with kings, they wanted a king of their own. God said I will give you a king, but you will be sorry. Israel spent the next 300 years under kings, some good, some bad. They spent the following 800 years under foreign rule and in exile longing for God to be their king. Prophets predicted the coming of a political and military messiah who would save their country from domination by foreign empires and bring them back under the rule of God. This is the Kingdom of God that Jesus was talking about. He did not claim to be the messiah. Jesus came to Israel to announce that God was coming to claim his own. The rest of us only get the scraps that fall from the table, but there are many choice morsels that fall from this banquet.

And yet, this interpretation does not fit all of Jesus' references to God's kingdom. He says that we should seek his kingdom and his righteousness first. The best definition may be in Jesus' instructions on how to pray: "your kingdom come, your will be done on earth as it is in heaven." *If* people would do God's will on earth, that *would be* God's kingdom. It wouldn't matter who was king, emperor, or president; that's just government. The *ruler* would be God.

Acts of the Apostles

Luke wrote *Acts of the Apostles* right after his account of the gospel, Part II of his book. While the book of *Luke* addresses the life and ministry of Jesus, the book of *Acts* records the ministry of the apostles Peter, Paul, and others during the 30 years that had elapsed from the death of Jesus to the writing of the book. Most likely, his accounts came directly from the apostles Peter, Paul and other apostles. It is written as a straightforward historical account. The first chapters of the book describe the ministry of Peter and other apostles. And a new character is introduced: the Holy Spirit. Peter's interpretation of this is that the last days are upon them. According to Peter, "Jesus of Nazareth was a *man* accredited by God to you by miracles, wonders, and signs, which God did among you through him." He said, "Repent and be baptized, in the name of Jesus Christ for the forgiveness of your sins. And you will receive the gift of the Holy Spirit." And "Repent and turn to God, so that your sins may be wiped out, that times of refreshing may come from the Lord." This is the same message of repentance that Jesus preached.

Believers devoted themselves to the apostles' teaching, to the fellowship, to the breaking of bread, to praising God, and to prayer. In part because they believed the last days were upon them, they had everything in common. They sold their possessions and goods and gave to anyone as he had need. Something happens in the book of *Acts* that didn't happen in any of the gospels. When a man named Ananias and his wife

Sapphira kept part of the proceeds from the sale of a piece of property and presented the remainder to the apostles, Peter accused Ananias of lying to the Holy Spirit and to God and Ananias fell down and died. The same thing happened to his wife Sapphira. King Herod died a mysterious death, but it is possible that Luke's Galatian mind attributed supernatural causes to the perfectly natural death of Herod. In the case of Ananias, Peter didn't say "in the name of Jesus Christ [or the Holy Spirit] die", but he made the accusation and the result followed. Seeing this result, Peter didn't avoid this circumstance in the future. On the contrary, he is more explicit with Sapphira and the same result follows. The end result is that great fear seized the whole church and all who heard about these events.

Let's imagine Jesus in similar circumstances. Let's say when Jesus told the rich young man to sell everything he had and give to the poor, then follow him, the man said, "OK". He went away, sold everything and gave most of the proceeds to the poor, but kept part for himself, then reported to Jesus. Jesus would know what he had done. To others he might describe him as an unfruitful seed sown among thorns, but how would he have handled the situation at the time? When faced with a sinful Samaritan woman, Jesus said, "Go, call your husband and come back." She replies that she has no husband. Jesus disarms her with the truth. He says, "You are right when you say you have no husband…you have had five husbands, and the man you now have is not your husband." The end result of this encounter was that the woman and many more of the Samaritans from that town became believers. Jesus set the woman up for success; he didn't attack her. Let's rearrange some of Peter's words into something Jesus might have said. "Did the land belong to you before it was sold?" Jesus would have waited for a response, not fired two more questions at Ananias as Peter did. Ananias, realizing that Jesus knew what he had done, would probably have repented and brought the rest of the money. End result: Ananias and Sapphira would have repented and lived to work with the apostles, and the apostles would have had more money to meet the needs of those within their number. In the years immediately after the crucifixion, the words and actions of the disciples are already beginning to deviate from the way of Jesus.

The book of Acts continues with the history of the apostles. The disciples chose seven men to take care of the physical needs of widows and others in need within their numbers, and they were ordained by prayer and laying on of hands. The high priest and the Sadducees persecuted the apostles. Stephen, one of the seven, was stoned, and all the rest of the believers were scattered throughout Judea and Samaria. Peter said that "God ... accepts men from every nation who fear him and do what is right ... God anointed Jesus of Nazareth with the Holy Spirit and power, and he went around doing good and healing ... because God was with him." This message was spreading through the country: Jesus went around doing good and healing because God was with him.

Enter Paul

A third of the way into the book of Acts, Saul (Paul) enters the scene and immediately after he is converted from a persecutor to a baptized follower of Jesus, he begins to preach that Jesus is the "Son of God". Not once does James use this phrase to describe Jesus in his book. In Mark's description of the baptism of Jesus, God says "You are my Son, whom I love; with you I am well pleased." One way to interpret this is that Jesus is God's son in the same sense that we are all, as God's creatures, sons and daughters of God, and that the emphasis here is on "*with whom I am well pleased.*" Finally, hundreds of years after his last prophet with whom he was well pleased, is a man who does and says His will. The only other times Mark uses the phrase "Son of God" it comes from the mouths of evil spirits and a (Roman) centurion at Jesus' death. In the book of Matthew, after Jesus walked on the water the disciples said, "You are the Son of God." The fact that Jesus makes no comment on this makes this response seem like a later addition to the story. When Jesus asked the disciple Peter who he was, Peter responded with "You are the Christ, the Son of the living God" and Jesus replied that this was revealed to him by his Father. All three of the earliest gospels record this exchange, but Matthew's is the only one that includes the words "Son of God" in Peter's response. I believe that these words were added by a later editor.

Luke uses the phrase "Son of God" in his opening story of the virgin birth, the baptism, and the transfiguration, the stories that are least likely to have come from eyewitnesses. Jesus, although he frequently referred to God as his Father (and also as your Father), always referred to himself as the "Son of man", i.e. mortal, and a particularly ironic choice of words for those who believe in the divine paternity of Jesus. The phrase "Son of man" is used a lot in the Old Testament, but almost all of the occurrences are in the book of Ezekiel. It is how the LORD referred to the prophet Ezekiel. Most of the other times "son of man" means either the same as or less than man. There is only one instance where it means someone greater than men. Jesus did not preach that he was the Son of God, in fact he strongly forbid his disciples to tell anyone that he was. Why? Was this out of some false sense of modesty? Was it in fear for his life? Would a son of God have to fear for his life? No, Paul was preaching what Jesus told his disciples not to preach, not only because it wasn't true, but because it was incompatible with Jesus' own monotheistic faith.

In the book of Acts Paul struck a man blind "for a time". The governor had sent for Paul because he wanted to hear the word of God. His attendant Elymas opposed Paul. Paul accused the attendant of being a child of the devil and said, "You are going to be blind, and for a time you will be unable to see." Immediately he became blind. Now let's imagine Jesus with Elymas. When Jesus faced vocal opposition while he was teaching, his response was "Be quiet! Come out of him!" We are told that the evil spirit shook the man violently and came out of him with a shriek and news of Jesus spread quickly over the whole region of Galilee. When Paul struck the man blind

31

we are told that the governor believed and was amazed at the teaching about the Lord. We are not told what became of Elymas after his time of blindness. The governor was amazed, but was this really teaching about the Lord that Paul gave him? Or was it a circus sideshow designed to attract attention at the expense of the attraction? Paul went around speaking and traveling, and occasionally God confirmed the message by enabling him to do miraculous signs and wonders. He often displayed a haughty attitude. "Since you [the Jews] reject it and do not consider yourselves worthy of eternal life, we [Barnabus and Paul] now turn to the Gentiles. For this is what the Lord has commanded us: 'I have made you a light for the Gentiles, that you may bring salvation to the ends of the earth,'" adopting Isaiah's prophecy as their own. Paul's attitude is far from that of Jesus.

In the book of *Acts,* the apostle James speaks with the voice of reason and practicality: We should not make it difficult for the Gentiles who are turning to God, instead we should give them basic rules to follow. Paul had such a sharp disagreement with Barnabas, who had been his advocate and companion from the beginning of his ministry, that they parted company. Paul was the kind of man who had trouble getting along with his closest companion.

Let us contrast the words and behavior of Jesus when he was brought before the Sanhedrin (the Jewish High Council) and Paul when it was his turn. The night before his arrest, Jesus spent hours praying to God, "Not what I will, but what You will." Jesus remained silent before the Sanhedrin and

32

only when he was asked a direct question by the high priest did he give a one-sentence answer. The next day he was crucified. When Paul was brought before the Sanhedrin, he was the first to speak. The high priest ordered those standing near Paul to strike him on the mouth, and Paul's response was "God will strike you, you whitewashed wall! You sit there to judge me according to the law, yet you yourself violate the law by commanding that I be struck!" When he was told he was speaking to the high priest he decided to retract his words, but he continued to incite a dispute between the Sadducees and Pharisees that were present. He was transferred, tried, held for two years, had another hearing, and appealed to Caesar. He had a third hearing. King Agrippa accused him of being out of his mind, but says, "This man is not doing anything that deserves death or imprisonment...This man could have been set free if he had not appealed to Caesar." Paul went to Rome, arranged to speak to many of the leaders of the Jews, and he lived there and preached his gospel for two years before his trial.

Galatians – The Breach

The book of Galatians was actually written before some of the other New Testament books we have discussed, but it makes no attempt to be a historical or factual account. It is an evangelistic letter written by Paul after he had spent about 12 years living among pagans. It starts out as a desperate tirade, for by this point Paul's beliefs and teachings had widely diverged from those of Peter and the other apostles. Paul has replaced part of the teachings of Jesus, Peter, and the other apostles with his own. This is the first we hear that Jesus gave himself for our sins to rescue us. Paul's tone is very defensive. "Even if an angel from heaven should preach a gospel other than the one we preached to you, let him be eternally condemned!" Does this sound like a man who speaks with the confidence that his message is directly from Jesus or like the wizard of Oz saying, "Pay no attention to that man behind the curtain"?

Paul describes his quarrel with the apostles Peter, James, and Barnabus. Two of the points of contention seem to be eating with gentiles and circumcision, with which we are not concerned. The third item of contention is the law. In Mark, Jesus said "You have let go of the commands of God and are holding on to the traditions of men."[a] And "I have not come to abolish [the law or the prophets] but to fulfill them." In Galatians, Paul says "we may be justified [made right with God] by faith in Christ and not by observing the law because by observing the law no one will be justified."[b] And "After beginning with the spirit, are you now trying to attain your goal by human effort?" He seems to deride even using the law as a guide to right living. He says, "I plead with you brothers (Galatians) become like me *for I became like you.*"[c] I became like you. I left my Jewish roots and became like you, the

---

[a] 7:8
[b] 2:16
[c] verse 4:12

34

pagans of Galatia. He says "You who are trying to be justified by law have been alienated from Christ; you have fallen away from grace, but by faith we eagerly *await…the righteousness* for which we hope."[a]

God gave Moses the law that we might know what is pleasing to God and what is abhorrent to Him. Jesus studied the law and the scriptures for 30 years. He interpreted law and taught scripture for 3 years, give or take. He sought out those who were not in compliance with the law to bring them back to God and to ways that are pleasing to God. He said not everyone who calls him Lord will enter the kingdom of heaven, but only the one who does what his heavenly Father wants. I think the ones who would be alienated from Jesus would be those who make no attempt to search out what is pleasing to God, but "await…righteousness" as if it were going to drop from the sky into their lives.

Christians tend to hear and use the name Jesus and the title Christ interchangeably, but on closer reading, we see that the oldest books of the New Testament speak of God, "the Lord", and Jesus. The gospels of Mark, Matthew, and Luke are about Jesus. Paul's later letters and all later books of the New Testament are about Christ. Paul is writing, not about Jesus of Nazareth, but about the character Christ who he has only loosely based on Jesus. The religion of Christianity was not built upon Jesus of Nazareth or his ministry. It was built

---

[a] verse 5:4

upon the character Christ – a composite built from the historical expectations of Jews and the educated and Pagan-influenced pen of Paul of Tarsus. Christians tend to hear and use the titles Christ and Son of God interchangeably, but the Messiah (in Greek, *Christ*) that Jews were expecting was not the "son of God" but a human, political ruler. Jews were never expecting God to have a son. Only Pagan gods had sons. It was Paul who declared that the Christ was also the son of God.

Jesus said to enter through the narrow gate. The gate is wide and the road is broad that leads to destruction, and many enter through it. But the gate is small and the road that leads to life is narrow, and only a few find it. Paul ripped out part of the wall to try to get as many as he could in; in doing so he didn't get more into the kingdom of God, he only made it harder for those looking for the narrow gate to find it. Jesus had clearly marked the way to the gate. Paul removed his directions.

Throughout the first fifteen hundred years of Biblical writings, people were expected to obey the commandments of the Bible and to pay for any sins with sacrifices. There are only a couple of references to someone else paying the price of the community's sins in the entire Old Testament. If anything, the standard in the gospels is even higher. In Matthew, Jesus said, "men will have to give account on the day of judgment for every careless word they have spoken."[a] The books of the

---

[a] 12:36

New Testament present the evolving tradition of sacrifice, offering their updated alternatives to sacrifice: Matthew – mercy, Mark – love, Romans – your bodies as living sacrifices, holy and pleasing to God, and finally Hebrews – praise, do good and share with others because God is pleased with such sacrifices. The Hebrew God of 30 AD was not looking for a human or semi-divine sacrifice to atone for the sins of humans. In Galatians, Paul reaches the peak of his tirade in verse 5:12. After that he apparently spent some time in prayer and gives much better advice.

Corinthians – He Died for our Sins

Paul's first letter to the Corinthians starts out with 5 chapters of godly advice. In verse 5:7 he introduces a new identity of Jesus – "our Passover lamb…sacrificed". The implications of this are profound. He is saying that by painting your household with the name of Christ the angel of death will spare you and your household. Jesus himself made no such claims. Paul writes, "keeping God's commands is what counts."[a] Had he reformed in the time that passed since he wrote Galatians? In Chapter 7, Paul specifies that some of his writings come from the Lord, others come from him. That he would be so explicit here implies that the same is true throughout his writings, but many Christians believe that

---

[a] verse 7:19

unless it specifically says it's from him, that it is from the Lord. He says women should remain silent in the churches. They are not allowed to speak, but must be in submission, as the law says.[a] In other passages he holds the law in contempt, but here he finds it in his interests to uphold the law. Jesus had no problem teaching and holding conversations with women.

Paul calls the cup of the last supper a participation in the blood of Christ. He calls the bread that we break a participation in the body of Christ.[b] The account of the Lord's supper in 1 Corinthians was the first one written down. Remember, Paul was not an eyewitness; he received the tradition of the last supper from the early church. Jesus' passing of the torch of his insight, understanding, knowledge, his very essence is here transformed into a bloody sin offering. Paul's interpretation here helped to form the theology of the church and found its way into the later gospels.

In 1 Corinthians, about 25 years after Jesus was crucified, Paul writes for the first time the central tenet of Christianity, that Christ died for our sins according to the scriptures.[c] He was probably referring to Isaiah 52:13-53:12. It is impossible to read this passage and not see that this is the Christ Paul preaches. There are two things that I would like to point out. God (through Isaiah) is describing his *servant*, not his *son*. God, having neither goddess or mortal as a wife (as

---

[a] verse 14:34
[b] verse 10:16
[c] verse 15:3

the gods of the ancients did) knew that he would never conceive a son, but among the children of Israel, there would be one who would do his will, one with whom he would be well-pleased. The only verses in the passage that do not describe the life of Jesus described in the Bible are "we considered him stricken by God, smitten by him and afflicted"[a] and "though the LORD makes his life a guilt offering, he will see his offspring and prolong his days."[b] This points to a resurrection life not of 40 days of ministry then ascension to heaven but 20 years of family life. When Christians rely so heavily on every other word of this passage, it is hard to discount these two pieces of the puzzle that don't fit with our traditional understanding.

That scripture would make Jesus the suffering servant, but does it make him the Messiah, the Christ? The prophet Jeremiah wrote that the days are coming when God will raise up a righteous branch from David's line, "a king who will reign wisely and do what is just and right in the land. In his days Judah will be saved and Israel will live in safety."[c] Jesus was never a king who reigned wisely keeping Israel safe from her enemies. Malachi describes the Messiah as the coming judge who "will be like a refiner's fire or a launderer's soap. He will sit as a refiner and purifier of silver; he will purify the Levites and refine them like gold and silver. Then the Lord will have

---

[a] verse 53:4
[b] verse 53:10
[c] verse 23:5

men who will bring offerings in righteousness". Jesus talked about the day of judgment as still being in the future. He did not burn off the dross or wash out the dirt. These verses are clearly not referring to Jesus' earthly life.

The Resurrection of the Body

In 1 Corinthians, Paul, in his roundabout way, explains the resurrection of the dead.[a] In Paul's time (and in the areas where Paul lived and traveled) there were people who believed in the immortality of the soul and there were people who believed that death was the end, that did not believe in the resurrection of the body. Paul is addressing those who did not believe in the resurrection of the body as a general principle. He says, in effect, there must be resurrection of the body because Christ was raised from the dead. Then, worried that some would reach the opposite conclusion – that since there is no resurrection of the body then Christ must not have been raised either – he lists the ramifications of that possibility:

- Our preaching is useless
- Your faith is futile, useless
- The apostles are to be found false witness
- You are still in your sins
- Those who have "fallen asleep" are lost

---

[a] 1 Corinthians 15:12

I'm not sure how he thought this proved his case, but it's all he had. But, he says, Christ was the first one to be raised, and when he comes he will cause the resurrection of those who belong to him, raised in a heavenly, imperishable, "spiritual" body.

Romans - By all possible means

In the opening verses of Paul's letter to the Romans, he says that Jesus was declared to be the Son of God by his resurrection from the dead (notably not by anything about his birth or baptism). So if the resurrection of Jesus declared him to be the Son of God, and all who belong to him are to be resurrected, that would make all who belong to Jesus sons of God. And in fact in his letter to the Galatians Paul says "you are all sons of God." Paul was pretty loose with the language that many take so literally.

In his letter to the Romans Paul declares that God will give eternal life to those who persist in doing good, and there will be trouble and distress for every human being who does evil[a], and he says "It is those who obey the law who will be declared righteous"[b]. This directly contradicts what he wrote to the Galatians in verse 2:16 four years earlier. In Romans verse 2:26 he says, "If those who are not circumcised keep the law's requirements, will they not be regarded as though they

---

[a] 2:7
[b] verse 2:13

were circumcised?" but in verse 3:20 Paul says no one will be declared righteous by observing the law. What are we to make of this man who not only contradicts what he wrote four years earlier, but also what he wrote one chapter earlier? I inscribed this book with a quote from Daniel Boorstin "I write to discover what I think." But as I discover it I try to go back and make my writing consistent. Paul would not have the luxury to go back and change a letter he had written and sent, but you would think he would be consistent within one letter.

Paul was a man who tailored his words to his audience. The church in Rome consisted of both Jews and gentiles and the entire letter would have been read to his original audience. He includes what both Jews and gentiles would have wanted to hear. He seems to hope each will hear what he wants and ignore the message intended for the other part of the audience. To understand Paul we need to look at what he wrote in his first letter to the Corinthians. "To the Jews I became like a Jew, to win the Jews. To those under the law I became like one under the law, so as to win those under the law. To the weak I became weak, to win the weak. I have become all things to all men so that by all possible means I might save some."[a] Jesus spoke the uncompromising words of God. Some were attracted to it. Some were driven away from it. Paul's goal was to win converts by any means, even if that meant changing the message.

---

[a] verse 9:20

The Ultimate Sacrifice

In Romans Paul says, "*God* presented him [Jesus] as a sacrifice of atonement through faith in his blood."[a] How can God present a sacrifice to himself? What makes a sacrifice a sacrifice? It is not the death, but the ceremony of offering to the god. Whether Abraham in the desert, priests in the temple, or pagans to their gods, it is the presentation, the killing before the god that makes it a sacrifice. It was never acceptable to bring an animal that had died of natural causes or had already been slaughtered by a butcher. According to the ancient Hebrew law and tradition the sacrificial lamb's throat was to be slit and the blood allowed to flow in the Courtyard of the Priests within the temple. "For the life of the flesh is in the blood; and I have given it for you upon the altar to make reparations for yourselves; for it is the blood that makes reparation, by reason of the life."[b] Afterwards the sacrifice was burned or ceremonially eaten.

Jesus was unceremoniously executed by Roman authorities then buried. The only gospel writer who mentions blood is John, who said it spilled out on the execution grounds. How is it that Paul claims that this was a sacrifice to a God who 1000 years earlier declared he had no delight in sacrifices? The sacrifice acceptable to God is a broken spirit, a broken and contrite heart. Did this God suddenly develop a taste for

---

[a] verse 3:25
[b] Leviticus 17:11.

human or semi-divine flesh and blood? According the writers of the New Testament this "sacrifice" was neither burned nor ceremonially eaten by priests but buried in a tomb, and without the aid of any priests or ceremony, removed from the tomb, appeared here and there to various people, then rode a cloud to heaven. This is not a legal way to present a sacrifice.

All Have Sinned

In Romans, Paul outlines the concept that has come to be known as original sin. "The result of one trespass (Adam's) was condemnation for all men."[a] Paul invented this concept. Jesus said, "I have not come to call the righteous, but sinners." This implies that there *were* righteous people. Jesus left the 99 righteous people in search of the one lost sheep. Adam was created in the likeness of God. The likeness of God is not one bite away from sin. In Psalm 8, David asks, "What is man that God is mindful of him, and the son of man that He cares for him? Yet He has made him little less than God, and crowns him with glory and honor." God has made man little less than God. It is offensive to God to call all of his human creations sinners.

It is in his letter to the Romans that Paul wrote the often quoted "for all have sinned and fall short of the glory of God"[b]. Many churches seem to center their entire existence on this

---

[a] verses 5:12-19
[b] chapter 3:23

quote. They refer to all people (including themselves) as sinners and focus on the continuing nature of sin and the need to confess sins. This runs counter to the entire Bible, even Paul's writings. Psalm 26:9 says "Sweep me not away with sinners". Ecclesiastes says, "All share a common destiny – the righteous and the wicked, the good and the bad, the clean and the unclean, those who offer sacrifices and those who do not. As it is with the good man, so with the sinner"[a]. In Luke Jesus says, "There will be more rejoicing in heaven over one sinner who repents than over ninety-nine righteous persons *who do not need to repent.*"[b] In Romans, Paul says, "If, when we were God's enemies, we were reconciled to him through the death of his Son, how much more, having been reconciled, shall we be saved through his life!"[c]

The Bible is a guide for right living. It is an instruction book: This is how you should live. Jesus came to tell people they could break with the past and start a new life; you don't have to be the person you have been; you can be the person God always intended you to be. Paul's emphasis is definitely different than that of Jesus and the Old Testament, but even Paul didn't advocate the kind of groveling that some churches seem to specialize in. He wrote, "Those who live in accordance with the Spirit have their minds set on what the Spirit desires... the mind controlled by the Spirit is life and

---

[a] 9:2
[b] 15:7
[c] 5:10

peace...You, however, are controlled not by the sinful nature but by the Spirit, if the Spirit of God lives in you...because those who are led by the Spirit of God are sons of God."[a]

The Bible is not a negative book, beating people down and belittling them. It is an uplifting book, challenging us to live according to the positive examples, especially Jesus, and to learn from the mistakes of those recorded within its pages. It contains the keys to the Kingdom, so that you too can be a son or daughter of God. Churches that every week talk about man's sinful nature and the need to lean fully on the sacrifice of Jesus, teaching even the youngest children that there's something intrinsically wrong with them, do a terrible disservice to their congregations. Jesus said "You are the light of the world...let your light shine before men, that they may see your good deeds and praise your Father in heaven."[b] Who do these churches think they are to contradict what Jesus said? Jesus saw people as beautiful and had compassion on all of them. He never condemned anyone who came to him unless they had a self-righteous attitude. He only condemned those who were stuffed full of false piety and devoid of true spirituality.

In his letter to the Romans Paul discusses "eternal life".[c] Occasionally in both the Old Testament and in the earliest gospels there are vague references to souls after the death of

---

[a] Romans 8:5-14.
[b] Matthew 5:14.
[c] verses 5:20-21

the body, but the emphasis was always on this life. Jesus spoke of the resurrection of ordinary people, but in Matthew he said, "God is not the God of the dead but of the living."[a] It is not up to Paul to shift the emphasis of an entire religion from this life to the next.

1 and 2 Peter - Die to sin and live for righteousness

After the entrance of Paul into the book of Acts, Peter's preaching seems to change. B.P. (before Paul) Peter preached repentance, baptism, forgiveness. A.P. (after Paul) Peter preached that everyone who believes in Jesus receives forgiveness of sins. It seems that Paul was not only converting Gentiles, he was also converting apostles. Peter wrote his letters about 35 years after Jesus was killed. They combine the teachings of Jesus and the teachings of Paul. His first letter is summarized: "He himself bore our sins…so that we might die to sin and live for righteousness" and later "live…for the will of God."[b]

Many of Paul's writings do spread the teachings of Jesus. Much of what he wrote is valuable for spreading God's will. But his central theme that Christ died for our sins misses

---

[a] 22:32
[b] verse 2:24

the mark of what Jesus preached and what God spoke through the prophets.

John – I am the resurrection and the life

The book of John is said to have been written by John the disciple (and possibly cousin) of Jesus 60 years after the crucifixion of Jesus. If this is true, John the disciple must have been a very young man and John the writer must have been a very old man. We know very little of his life or actions after the crucifixion because he is barely mentioned in the book of Acts. He was certainly active in the early ministry in Jerusalem with the rest of the disciples, for thousands came to be followers of Jesus after his death and this could not have happened without the active participation by all the disciples. But after that he seems to have faded into a quiet life, sheltering the meaning and the words of Jesus in his heart until he became an old man and the words came spilling out. According to most scholars, what we have in the book of John is not a first edition, but a book which was refined by the church over a period of decades. In the final edition, "John" was a whole-hearted proponent of Jesus being the Son of God. He uses the phrase over and over again. He also seconds Paul's description of Jesus as the atoning sacrifice for our sins, but he makes it clear that this is for past sins.

Many are drawn to Christianity because of the promise of forgiveness. This is what Jesus offered. In John's first letter he writes, "No one who lives in him keeps on sinning. No one who continues to sin has either seen him or known him."[a] Biblical forgiveness allows you to break with the past and start a new life, but you are expected to break with the past and start a new life. In *A Place at the Table*, Mother Tessa Bielecki says, "The greater sin is actually the sin of omission, a failure to love, or a lack of charity...The worst sins are sins of pride, apathy, disregard for one's neighbor and for the rest of the world."[12] John preaches active love, sharing material possessions with those in need, loving all and hating none. He teaches walking as Jesus walked. The other three gospels record the actions and teachings of Jesus. John's emphasis is on who Jesus is: The Word, the lamb of God. These claims are not recorded in the earlier gospels. None of the other gospels have this interpretive analysis of "Who was that man?" They contain much less far-reaching titles such as rabbi, Lord of the Sabbath, and prophet.

John's Jesus says, "I am the bread of life... the shepherd... the way... the vine". The book of John is the latest gospel and most heavily influenced by Pauline theology, but if we dig below the editions, we can find the truth of what Jesus said. In the Hebrew tradition, the voice from the burning bush tells Moses that its name is "I Am what I Am". I Am is the divine, the Spirit of God. In Aramaic, bread is insight, understanding, knowledge. Wine is blood or essence.[13] So when Jesus says, "I Am the bread of life" he is saying that the

---

[a] verse 3:6

Spirit of God is insight for life. When he says, "I Am the vine; you are the branches. If a man remains in me and I in him, he will bear much fruit," he is saying that the Spirit of God is the vine, the source of man's blood, his essence; you are the branches. If a man remains in the Divine, and the Spirit remains in him, he will bear much fruit. These mystical sayings of Jesus defy pat translations, so they have escaped the simplistic interpretations of simpler statements such as "I and the Father are one." In 325 AD, the Council of Nicea decided that this meant that Jesus was of one substance with the Father. But to Jesus and his Aramaic speaking disciples it meant that the wine of the Holy vine flowed through his veins, not uniquely, but in the same way that it can flow through the veins of anyone who is in the Holy vine, bearing good fruit.

The Revelation to John

If John's gospel was not strange enough, 5 to 10 years later while in exile on the island of Patmos, he wrote the book of Revelation. If this is the same John, he had to have been very old and he writes that he was "in the Spirit" when this revelation was made to him. It is also possible that this book was written by a different John. At the beginning of the book, Jesus (through John) admonishes the seven churches for forsaking their first love, for holding to the teaching of Balaam, for tolerating Jezebel, etc., each of these relating to the sins of which those churches were guilty. John describes the terrible things that will happen to the earth, those who will survive it, and those who will be consumed in the process. As fractions of the world population are extinguished, John notes that the rest did not stop worshipping demons or idols, did not repent of murder, magic, sexual immorality or theft. There is a prophecy that sounds frighteningly like the United States, specifically New York City. In the end, the dead *are judged according to what they had done.* It says, "let him who does right continue to do right; and let him who is holy continue to be holy."[a]

When John falls at the feet of the angel to worship him, the angel commanded him not to worship him. "I am a fellow servant with you and with your brothers who hold to the testimony of Jesus. Worship God! For the testimony of Jesus is the spirit of prophecy."[b] The angel did not say, "Worship Jesus". He said "Worship God!" In the gospels, Jesus accepted the tears and perfume of Mary. And many called him "Lord" in the same way that a servant called his master Lord. In the book of Mark, Jesus said, "the Son of Man did not come to be served, but to serve". In Matthew, he said, "Worship the Lord your God, and *serve him only.*" In Luke's version of the triumphal entry, Jesus accepts the praise of the crowds, but in general, Jesus portrayed himself as a servant, washing the feet of his disciples, not as a king or a god that anyone should bow down to and worship. In the words of the scholar Marcus

---

[a] verse 22:11
[b] 19:10

51

Borg, Jesus was not christnocentric, but theocentric, pointing not to himself but to God.

Part Two:
The Way of Jesus

The early church (prior to Antioch) was called The Way. "Antioch saw Jesus as the model of what all humans could become. The church at Antioch was renowned for its followers' care for the poor, establishment of hospitals, and involvement in what would today be called a Social Gospel. This arose from their belief that humanity was capable of great good because God was capable of becoming one of us and of working through us."[14] These were the followers of Jesus uninfluenced by the Pagan elements that Paul added. The Christian church that Paul founded served to spread the word of God to millions of people all over the world. But the very elements that made it attractive to Mediterranean gentiles of the first century make it incompatible with much of the knowledge that has been gained in the past 100 years. A new version of the community of God, stripped of Pauline additions needs to be offered to minds and hearts of the 21st century. The closeness to God that Jesus offered brought power and meaning to his first followers. Power over physical infirmities. Meaning to ordinary lives. That power came at a price – total subjection to God and his laws and to the welfare of others.

In our modern Bibles, Mark 2:21-22 comes after verses 18-20, which leaves it out of context and hard to understand. These verses relate to verse 17. In that context they make much more sense. The Pharisees had asked of Jesus "Why does he eat with tax collectors and sinners?" Jesus replied that "It is not the healthy who need a doctor, but the sick. I have not come to call the righteous, but sinners." And he continued, "No one sews a patch of unshrunk cloth on an old garment. If he does, the new piece will pull away from the old, making the tear worse. And no one pours new wine into old wineskins. If he does, the wine will burst the skins, and both the wine and the wineskins will be ruined. No, he pours new wine into new wineskins." Verses 21-22 are part of his answer to the Pharisees about why he eats with sinners. If he poured his new teachings into old Pharisees both his teachings and the Pharisees would be ruined. No, he poured his teachings into those who were without a spiritual home.

In the same way, my desire is not to take anyone away from their Christian beliefs; my desire is to reach out to those who feel alienated from or not attracted to the Christian (Pauline) beliefs and doctrines. But, if any who have read this far were traditional Christians and are now feeling lost, let me say this. When I came to the beliefs that I now hold, I grieved for the part of me that died, for I had been wholeheartedly a Christian for many years. But I cling for support to the God who has always and still loves me.

Who was he?

So if Jesus was not the Messiah of Hebrew scripture, not the son of God, not a divine sacrifice, who was he? Jesus said, "Moses wrote about me." Moses was not known for his prophecy. The only thing he wrote which could refer to Jesus was Deuteronomy 18:15 "the LORD your God will raise up for you a prophet like me from among your own brothers. You must listen to him. The LORD said 'I will put my words in his mouth, and he will tell them everything I command him." I believe that Jesus was a prophet, blessed with the gifts of direct conversation with God and the ability to perform miracles, like Elijah and Elisha of the books of Kings in the Old Testament. The people of Jesus' time held that he was a prophet. In Matthew the crowds said, "This is the prophet Jesus from Nazareth of Galilee."[a] In Mark when those in his hometown rejected him he referred to himself as a prophet. "Only in his hometown, among his relatives and in his own house is a prophet without honor."[b] Even after his death, the disciples referred to him as a prophet. "About Jesus of Nazareth, he was a prophet, powerful in word and deed before God and all the people."[c]

In his book *Evidence that demands a Verdict*, Josh McDowell says when Jesus spoke in his own name (I say to you) instead of quoting Old Testament prophets, he was claiming authority of his words equal to God. McDowell doesn't seem to account for the possibility that Jesus was a

---

[a] 21:11
[b] 6:4
[c] Luke 24:19.

prophet, equal to Old Testament prophets many of whom spoke in their own names.

In Luke's gospel, Jesus unveiled his ministry by quoting the prophet Isaiah. "He has anointed me to preach good news to the poor...to proclaim freedom for the prisoners and recovery of sight for the blind, to release the oppressed, to proclaim the year of the Lord's favor." I am a preacher, an emancipator, an announcer. This is not a messianic prophecy. Jesus could have chosen any scripture to introduce himself. This is the one he chose.

All three of the synoptic gospels contain Jesus' discourse on "Whose son is the Christ?" In it, Jesus quotes a psalm of David and all but says the Christ is not a son of David. The Psalm speaks of the Lord as a ruler, warrior, and judge. Jesus says this is a prophetic psalm about the Christ. Jesus said David calls him "my Lord" so the Christ couldn't be David's son. Was he saying he could be the Christ even though he wasn't a son of David? Was he saying he couldn't be the Christ because he was a son of David? None of the gospel writers comment on this discourse because it doesn't fit in with their genealogies that show Jesus is a son of David through Joseph and their claims that he is the Christ. John's gospel contains a different version of this dialogue. In it people asked, "How can the Christ come from Galilee? Does not the Scripture say that the Christ will come from David's family and from Bethlehem, the town where David lived?" This seems to resolve the mystery of the other gospels, saying that Jesus was not a son of David, and incidentally, not born in Bethlehem.

There is a branch of Christianity that feels no necessity that the risen Christ be tied to the earthly Jesus. In his essay "The Irrelevancy of the Empty Tomb" Marcus Borg, a Christian, states that the pre-Easter Jesus was a Galilean woodworker of the peasant class and the post-Easter Jesus is King of kings and Lord of lords. I would counter that the pre-Easter Jesus was religious master, exorcist, healer, teacher, and preacher who didn't touch a hammer during his entire ministry. Prior to the book of Revelation, the title King of kings only referred to the Persian emperor, the Babylonian emperor, or God himself, and only God was ever referred to as Lord of lords. What is the basis on which these people support their idea of who the risen Christ is? For the moment, let's assume that Jesus did rise from the dead. That would mean God must have thought he was pretty extraordinary, but it would not change Jesus into something he had not been during his earthly life. His disciples certainly thought he was extraordinary.

In general, Americans at the dawn of the twenty-first century believe that each soul, each personality, comes to exist over a period between conception and some number of developmental years, a product of genetics and environment. We are not a society that believes in reincarnation. So the very premise that Christ always existed, then was born of Mary – theoretically with all of his physical traits coming from her, but all of his personality – mental, emotional, psychological – having always existed – is hard for me to accept. But there are many Christians who believe this, so of course, as an eternal soul, he would be the same after his resurrection. Jesus was a religious master whose followers hung on his every word and treated him with great respect. Great numbers of people asked him for healing. A few asked him for advice.

In the book of Mark, the only worship is the triumphal entry into Jerusalem, and to that Jesus has no reaction. No matter who he heals, there is no reaction of worship. What the woman with the jar of expensive perfume did is described as a beautiful thing, but not as worship. Through the first thirteen chapters of the book of Matthew, no one worshipped Jesus. There is only an isolated incident when Jesus walked on the water and saved Peter from drowning that those who were in the boat worshipped him saying, "You are the Son of God," but even the triumphal entry is downplayed. When the city asks, "Who is this?" the crowds answered, "This is Jesus, the prophet from Nazareth in Galilee." Jesus described the anointing at Bethany as preparation for burial. In Matthew Jesus said, "It is enough for the student to be like his teacher, and the servant like his master."[a] Jesus commanded us to be like him, not to worship him. Worship is an inappropriate response toward someone who only worshipped God. If the resurrection of Jesus fundamentally changed his role in the world, wouldn't he have told us? But he didn't. He reaffirmed what he preached during his whole ministry.

---

[a] 10:24

Who was he?

In Luke when Jesus healed a paralytic he "went home praising *God*. Everyone was amazed and gave praise to God." When he raised a widow's son "they were all filled with awe and praised God. 'A great prophet has appeared among us'". In Luke's telling of the anointing at Bethany, the woman continually kissed his feet. Jesus said, "She loved much." After Jesus healed the demon-possessed man in the Gerasenes he told him to "return home and tell how much God has done for you." When Jesus healed the boy with an evil spirit "they were all amazed at the greatness of God." The modern Pauline church constantly worships and praises Jesus, but when Jesus healed the crippled woman "she straightened up and praised God." When Jesus healed the ten lepers and one came back praising God, Jesus asked "Was no one found to return and give praise to God except this foreigner?" When the blind beggar received his sight he praised God and the people who saw it praised God. In Luke's telling of the triumphal entry the whole crowd began to praise God in loud voices for all the miracles they had seen. After Jesus was crucified, resurrected, and ascended, the disciples stayed continually at the temple praising God. In the book of Acts, after the crucifixion of Jesus, when Peter healed the crippled beggar he praised God.

Jesus was an agent of God. When he performed miracles, people gave God the praise. The personality that Jesus displayed on earth was a humble, serving spirit. He did not seek praise for himself. Any praise that might have come his way he deflected to God. If Christ is an eternal spirit, death and resurrection are just milestones. They would not change his eternal nature. If, since the resurrection of Christ, people experience something different from the humble, healing, teaching spirit of Jesus, it cannot be attributed to "the risen Christ." I think what has happened in the last 2000 years is that people are experiencing God in a way that they hadn't for hundreds of years before Jesus, perhaps ever. We must give credit for that to Jesus and all of his disciples, including Paul. But that doesn't mean we should say the experiences themselves are experiences of Christ or that we should worship him. We should, as Jesus and his contemporary followers did, give the glory to God, and God alone. Jesus was a man with a mission to seek out lost souls and return them to the fold of God. His disciples continued that mission for about 20 to 25 years, until Paul convinced them to spread a different message.

The author Dennis Harris, using either the assumption that the Gospels were eyewitness accounts of the life of Jesus, recording his actions and words as they happened or believing the Bible to be divinely inerrant, deduced that Jesus must have been a *Liar, Lunatic, or Lord*. Removing those assumptions we find new possibilities: that Paul was a liar, a lunatic, or he was mistaken. In the book *A Place at the Table*, Matthew Fox points out that "this zeroing in only on Jesus or the tradition of the second person of the Trinity is idolatry, a violation of the second commandment."

In the 1500's, Faustus Socinus said that the trinity was a "monstrosity, an imaginary fiction that was repugnant to reason and actually encouraged the faithful to believe in three separate gods."[15] The 16th century Italian church administrator

Menocchio "denied that Mary was a virgin, proposed that Jesus had been a prophet like many others who had appeared in the world, and criticized the sacraments..."[16] The church's response to his stance was to execute him in 1599.

In the 1800's Albrecht Ritschl saw the doctrine of the trinity "as a flagrant instance of Hellenization. It had corrupted the Christian message by introducing an alien layer of metaphysical concepts, derived from the natural philosophy of the Greeks, having nothing at all to do with the pristine Christian experience. The Greek Fathers were simply trying to make the Semitic concept of God work for them by expressing it in terms of their own culture."[17] It worked well for them. It doesn't work well for many 21st century Americans.

David Chidester's *Christianity – A Global History* traces Christianity from its earliest roots to the present day. In it, he says that "groups outside of [Jesus'] birthplace in Palestine increasingly understood Jesus as a deity who had descended into the world only to ascend to the heavens. In this respect, the Christ congregations followed a path that diverged from that of the Jesus movements, which had built their followings on recollections of the sayings and deeds of a teacher...As many historians have observed, Jesus might have been identified as the Christ, but Paul was the founder of Christianity...Paul combined a Jewish expectation of a resurrection of the dead from the earth with a Greco-Roman hope of achieving immortality in the air, merging both ... Positioning themselves between Jewish and Greek traditions, Christian intellectuals claimed elements from both, taking those elements out of context, and rearranged them into a new synthesis of religious doctrine."[18]

In the book *A Place at the Table*, Bishop John S. Spong points out that Paul (in the '50s) says that God proclaimed Jesus the son of God at the resurrection. Mark (in the '70s) says God poured out his spirit on him at his baptism. Matthew and Luke (in the '80s) said he was God from conception. John (in the '90s) said he was God from the foundation of the world.

Jesus said, "I am the way and the truth and the life." Through the centuries, other people who reached a state of enlightenment or oneness with God have made similar statements. Al-Hallaj, a member of the Sufi sect of Islam was "crucified like his hero Jesus. In his ecstasy, al-Hallaj had cried aloud: 'I am the truth!'"[19] In the gospel of John, the above quote of Jesus continues, "No one comes to the Father except through me." In the book *A Place at the Table*, Deepak Chopra explains that in Aramaic – the language Jesus spoke – the phrase translated "except by me" means something like "except by physical bodies which provide a vehicle to move from one reality to another." And Neil Douglas-Klotz says it means something like "except through another embodied 'I' connected to the ultimate 'I Am'"[20]. Combining the two of them: No one comes to the Father except through someone who is filled with the Holy Spirit. Hmm. Thought provoking. And completely different than the interpretation that no one can get close to God without going through Jesus. Jesus preached a gospel not based on calling his name, but on actively drawing near to his Father in heaven. "If you really knew me you would know my Father as well." Many Christians take this to mean that to know Jesus *is* to know the Father. I think he meant that if his disciples had been watching how he lived, they would know how to draw near to God themselves.

The Old Testament makes abundantly clear that God alone was the savior of his people and He is a jealous God. In Isaiah God says, "I, even I, am the LORD, and apart from me there is no savior. I have revealed and saved and proclaimed..."[a] He offered forgiveness of sins directly to His people. The Old Testament prophet Micah says, "Who is a God like you, who pardons sin and forgives the transgression of the remnant of his inheritance?"[b] In Exodus God says, "Do not worship any other god, for the LORD, whose name is Jealous, is a jealous God."[c] The Psalms say, "you, whose name is the LORD—you alone are the Most High over all the earth." "You alone are God."[d] The God of the Old Testament would not suffer to stand beside two other "persons" or for His people to offer their worship to any name other than his. Jesus was a prophet that we were to listen to and imitate, not a deity to be worshipped.

---

[a] 43:11
[b] 7:18
[c] 34:14
[d] 83:18 and 86:10

Who Was Paul?

So who is this man who is considered to be the author of half the books of the New Testament? Paul was a person "used by God to bring monotheism and the moral message of Judaism to the world, and to teach the world that the God discovered and worshipped by Jews was the only true God."[21] Paul was an educator, a missionary. He was not a prophet. He served to spread the word of God and knowledge of Jesus and his way. But he was not a mouthpiece for God, and his words and even his teachings should not be considered those of God. In his wisdom (or through God's inspiration), Paul wrote in his first letter to the Corinthians, "Now the body is not made up of one part but of many. If the foot should say, 'Because I am not a hand, I do not belong to the body,' it would not for that reason cease to be a part of the body ... Now you are the body of Christ, and each one a part of it. And in the church God has appointed first of all apostles, second prophets, third teachers...Are all apostles? Are all prophets? Are all teachers?"[a]

Now I would question Paul's ranking of spiritual gifts, but Paul was an apostle – one sent, a messenger. He was not a prophet. He did not claim to speak for God. He does not for that reason cease to be a part of the body of God's church, but we should not look to the foot to provide eyesight. That is what Christians do when they treat every word that Paul wrote

---

[a] 12:14-31

as Holy scripture. Paul was a messenger. He fulfilled his function of spreading the word of God, but he overstepped his authority when he ceased to spread God's word and commenced to create his own theology based on the beliefs and customs of the people around him. Feet should not claim to be able to see, and if they do, the hands should not believe them and act on their "sight".

We should look to the prophets to hear the word of God and speak it to us. Because two bishops and a scholar of the fourth century declared at the foundation of the orthodox church that the feet could see and we should follow where they lead does not mean that they could or we should. And it certainly does not mean that no subsequent eyes would ever see. Paul served God's purpose. But let us move on and stop being deluded by Paul's "vision". Let us look for guidance to Jesus, the prophets of the Old Testament, and to the many inspired writers since Jesus. Let us break free of the definition declared by the fourth century church that 27 books were the word of God and all other writings are not. Those 27 books do contain the word of God. They also contain many words that are not of God, and there are many other writings that also contain the word of God.

If God was declaring a new covenant – a new testament – don't you think that declaration would have come from the mouth of Jesus – not from the pen of Paul? The writers of the gospels put the words "This is my blood of the covenant, which is poured out for many" coming from the mouth of Jesus at the last supper. But I challenge you to read every word from

Mark, Matthew, and Luke and without resorting to the writings of Paul try to find an actual statement of what that covenant was. What I find is, "If you want to enter life, obey the commandments…do not murder, do not commit adultery, do not steal, do not give false testimony, honor your mother and father, and love you neighbor as yourself…If you want to be perfect, go, sell your possessions and give to the poor, and you will have treasure in heaven. Then come, follow me."

Jesus handpicked the original twelve disciples. They were a diverse lot, but with the possible exception of Judas Iscariot, they were good men, motivated to do what was right. Before Paul was converted he was a serious threat to the young and growing church. God struck down the pride in this man and he underwent three days of blindness and fasting and several days talking with the disciples. The outcome of this was that he ceased to persecute the church, and began to preach *about* Jesus, not what Jesus preached. While he probably couldn't have been successful in completely squashing the nascent church, he was fantastically successful in diverting the church from its original mission.

In the second century Clementine *Homilies*, Peter says to Paul "How can you be qualified to teach the gospel just because you had a vision? If you say it is possible, then why did Jesus go through the trouble of spending a whole year with us [the twelve]? And how can we believe you? If he really appeared to you, why do you teach precisely the opposite of what he taught?"[22] Paul "wasn't even interested in Jesus; just in his own idea of the Christ."[23]

The Second Coming

The writers of the New Testament clearly expected the kingdom of God (or the second coming of Christ) within their generation. In Mark, Jesus said, "Some who are standing here will not taste death before they see the kingdom of God come with power."[a] He said, "This generation will certainly not pass away until all these things have happened."[b] In Matthew he said, "You will not finish going through the cities of Israel before the Son of Man comes."[c] Other verses in the book of Matthew also put these things within Jesus' generation. In Luke he says, "Some who are standing here will not taste death before they see the kingdom of heaven."[d] In John, Jesus said "If I want him (John) to remain alive until I return, what is that to you?"[e] 2000 years later we still await his return.

Let's separate the kingdom of God from the second coming of Christ. Let's say that when Jesus spoke of the kingdom of God coming with power he was expecting that his ministry (and that of his disciples) would be successful – that people would hear his message and change their ways – God's will being done on earth as it is in heaven. If this happened, the transformation would spread rapidly; before they had finished going through the cities of Israel, Jesus would be

---

[a] 9:1
[b] verse13:30
[c] 10:23
[d] 9:27
[e] 21:22

67

crowned as earthly king, and the kingdom of God would have no end. Perhaps Jesus miscalculated people's reaction to Truth coming to this world. People preferred darkness to the truth. The people living in darkness have seen a great light. He has proclaimed freedom for the prisoners and recovery of sight for the blind, he has released the oppressed and proclaimed the year of the Lord's favor and people said, "No, thank you. We prefer living in darkness, as prisoners, blind and oppressed." This was a reaction that was not foreseen. How do you reach out to a people that doesn't want to be reached? It's not that they were happy the way they were, but they were comfortable. They knew what to expect.

God always knew that there would have to be someone to prepare the way before the Lord came. He sent John the Baptizer, and according to Mark, "the whole Judean countryside and all the people of Jerusalem went out to him. Confessing their sins, they were baptized by him in the Jordan River."[a] And Jesus "had compassion on them, because they were like sheep without a shepherd. So he began teaching them many things." But he was not what the Pharisees were expecting. The Pharisees, more than everyone else, were comfortable with the way things were and threatened by what Jesus offered. Jesus didn't fast. He did what was unlawful on the Sabbath. He ate without washing his hands. And they feared him "because the crowd was amazed at his teaching."

---

[a] 1:5

Once they had the shepherd arrested, the sheep were easily led to call for the release of the prisoner Barabbas and the crucifixion of Jesus, king of the Jews. John the Baptist prepared the people, but he didn't eliminate the power of the status quo.

Deepak Chopra, in the book *A Place at the Table*, describes "Christ" as a state of awareness that we could all aspire to, the essence of unity and compassion. He describes the second coming as a critical mass of people in "Christ Consciousness" resulting in the world changing. In other words, the kingdom of God is still at hand. All we have to do is join it.

Why did the earliest disciples come to think of their master and teacher as the Messiah? Describing Jesus as the Christ necessitated a second coming of Christ (which had never been part of earlier prophecy) because Jesus didn't do what the Christ was expected to do. The prophet Daniel wrote, "From the issuing of the decree to restore and rebuild Jerusalem until the Anointed One, the ruler, comes, there will be seven 'sevens,' and sixty-two sevens."[a] The issuing of the decree to restore and rebuild Jerusalem was in about 450 BC. Seven times seven years plus sixty-two times seven years equals 483 years. 483 years later takes us to about 33 AD, around the time that Jesus lived. Students of prophecy were looking for the Anointed One. Daniel continues, "After sixty-two 'sevens' the

---

[a] 9:25

Anointed One will be cut off and will have nothing. The people of the ruler who will come will destroy the city and the sanctuary."[a] Tradition holds that Jesus' earthly ministry lasted about three years, but in going through all four gospels, I could find no evidence for the passage of that much time. The evidence points more to a ministry that lasted about "sixty-two weeks" after which he was cut off. The rest of the prophecy was fulfilled when the people of the Roman ruler who came destroyed the temple in 70 AD after Jesus was crucified.

If Christ Came Today

Jesus told many parables about how God reached out to his own people (the Jews), but since they rebuffed him he went out into the world and reached out to gentiles, but not all gentiles; only those clothed in righteousness are welcome in the kingdom of God.[b] The Jews were the first to discover the one supreme God. Or God first reached out to the Jews. Or God was there in the beginning with man, and Abraham and his descendants were the only ones not to go astray. God is now available to all people. We live in an age of communication and transportation that people 200 years ago could never have dreamed of. The United States is an open country where all ideas are freely exchanged. Transformation of society is possible now as it has never been possible before.

------

[a] 9:26
[b] Matthew 22:11

If Christ Came Today

If Christ came today, not to usher in the end of the world, but as he did 2000 years ago, complete with healing power and exposition of divine principles, the news would spread faster than wildfire. Society is much different than it was 2000 years ago. How would people react? If a child who had been living with severe, life-threatening birth defects for the first five years of his life was restored to perfect health and there were other healing and non-healing miracles, how would people react? This is not the kind of thing that could be denied. Besides all the people who knew him there would be extensive medical documentation of his condition, surgeries, medications, etc. Many would want the benefit of complete healing at no cost. At no cost. Few would be willing to make changes to their lifestyle as advocated by Jesus. Some people may be willing to change what they believe; a much smaller number may be willing to change how they live. Those who call themselves atheists might become agnostics. Those who call themselves agnostics might become believers. Those who call themselves Christians might assess their lives to see if they are living as Jesus would have them live. I think that our comfort would have to be removed before the masses would be willing to embrace a new lifestyle. The shock could be economic or violent, but it would have to be profound. If some sort of shock occurred before Christ arrived, perhaps the transformation would be more complete. What of those who follow other religions? Perhaps a new Christ would bring reconciliation between religions whose followers have seen their beliefs as irreconcilable with others.

A significant portion of Jesus' ministry was devoted to rectifying religion. Jesus did not have much contact with religions other than Judaism, so his teaching focused on what he knew best. Jesus deemphasized fasting, Sabbath, cleanliness laws, Pharisees, and Sadducees, and opposed public prayer and selling of sacrifices. He endorsed the temple tax. He shared his wisdom on all of these aspects of organized religion. Other aspects of religion he did not comment on, but followed: reading scripture and teaching in the synagogues, private prayer, celebrating the Passover. Jesus evaluated the "church" of his day and cursed what did not belong and blessed what did belong in true religion. Two thousand years of rituals and doctrines have grown up since Jesus was here on earth. Jewish Pharisees don't exist anymore. Christian and Muslim "Pharisees" do. There are many who call themselves religious who are quick to say others are from the devil, who are looking for signs, who are confined by the written scriptures. A new Christ would have much to evaluate and condemn. A new Christ would find plenty of people who shut the kingdom of heaven in men's faces, plenty who travel over land and sea to win a single convert, leaving him worse than before, plenty who are so concerned with the literal inerrancy of the Bible that they fail to see how self-indulgent this belief is.[a] There are also many who long to break free from these confines, but fear being "put out of the synagogue" by religious leaders.[b] But

---

[a] Matt. 23:13-15
[b] Luke 17:20

according to Jesus' brother, "religion that is pure and undefiled before God and the Father is this: to visit orphans and widows in their affliction, and to keep oneself unstained from the world."[a]

We decry the fickleness of crowds who would shout, "Blessed is he who comes in the name of the Lord!" on Palm Sunday and "Crucify him!" on Good Friday, but today the media does the same thing. Yesterday's darling is today's scandal. People love to see the mighty brought low. If Christ came today with the promise of healing, he would threaten the huge health care industry. With his advocacy of simple lifestyle, he would threaten the entire economy of the United States. You don't need a big house, expensive furniture and decorating. You don't need a fancy car or SUV. Your kids don't need the latest toys and you don't need the latest fashions and electronic gadgets. You don't need to go on expensive vacations or eat in fancy restaurants. He would have many enemies. What seemed like good ideas on Sunday could mean you could be out of a job on Friday. I doubt he would survive more than "sixty-two weeks". Of course, that would be if he were assassinated. If he went through our legal system, even if he were sentenced to death on some trumped up charge he could preach and minister for the next 30 years from prison while on appeal.

---

[a] James 1:27.

Actually, he might find the inside of a prison the very best place to start to transform the world. He would be much more likely to make friends than enemies inside prison. For the most part, prisons are a drain on government funds, not a private industry operating to make a profit. And any influence that improves the behavior of inmates would be welcome. The inmates themselves might welcome anyone who would befriend hardened criminals. Jesus sought the company of sinners because they are the ones "in need of a doctor". A psychologist, layman, or minister might start a prison ministry by asking inmates, "How did you end up here?" Jesus would likely skip that step and proceed directly to "Your sins are forgiven." He had the power to transform lives. He released those who were in bondage to sin. He gave people the desire and the strength to follow the commandments. From there they would need family and job training and placement to become productive members of society.

Imagine if prisons took in criminals and released contributing members of society. They would work themselves out of a job instead of always having to build more facilities to warehouse criminals. What would a city be without crime and criminals? Perhaps without a fear of crime and criminals people would become more open to getting involved in one another's lives.

Another view of Jesus

In 1947 the Dead Sea scrolls were discovered and with them a view of the Essene sect of Judaism. Jesus had much in common with the Essenes. There are some who claim that he was an Essene. Let's explore this possibility. Jesus was renowned for his healing ability and an occasional raising from the dead. He preached piety. He called God his father. He never married. Some of Jesus' hardest sayings make much more sense from the Essene point of view. In a brief inquiry into the way of life of the Essenes, I discovered that the forty day fast and temptation of Jesus would have been a typical life examination for a rising member of the sect. Essenes were to simplify everything within themselves to become one with their ideal in order to keep their bond with God alive and pure. This was the source of all healing. Solitude was regarded as sacred, because when one was alone, one was in the presence of God. Jesus was always seeking solitude with God.

Essenes refuse to swear oaths, believing every word they speak to be stronger than an oath. Jesus said, "Do not swear at all, either by heaven, for it is the throne of God, or by the earth, for it is his footstool, or by Jerusalem, for it is the city of the great King. And do not swear by your head, for you cannot make one hair white or black. Let what you say be simply 'Yes' or 'No'; anything more than this comes from evil."[a] Essenes do not marry. Jesus didn't marry and

---

[a] Matthew 5:34.

discouraged others from marrying. Jesus said, "others have renounced marriage because of the kingdom of heaven. The one who can accept this should accept it."[a] Essenes considered fellow members brothers but strangers (outsiders) unclean. When Jesus' mother and brothers were calling for him, looking for him, he said of those seated around him, "Here are my mother and my brothers!"

The Essenes were Jews united by mutual affection and by their efforts to cultivate a completely moral life. They were devoted students of the healing of diseases and spent their time and their activity healing the sick. Jesus devoted a great portion of his time and efforts to healing the sick. They were ardent students of the properties of stones. Could they turn stones into bread? The devil said Jesus could turn stones into bread. Is that how he fed the 5000? Essenes believed that their souls are immortal. The souls of the wicked would be relegated to a dark pit full of unending chastisement.[24] Jesus preached that the soul was immortal and that the souls of the wicked would be cast into the outer darkness where there would be weeping and gnashing of teeth.

There was a rule forbidding Essenes to reveal the Teaching to people who were not prepared to receive it. The law of silence and discernment was strictly enforced. Jesus said, "Do not give pearls to pigs for fear that they will trample them underfoot and turn towards you to devour you."[b] He told

---

[a] Matthew 19:11
[b] Matthew 7:6.

the twelve disciples and others around him, "The secret of the kingdom of God has been given to you. But to those on the outside everything is said in parables so that, 'they may be ever seeing but never perceiving, and ever hearing but never understanding; otherwise they might turn and be forgiven!'"[a] "Consider carefully how you listen. Whoever has [understanding] will be given more; whoever does not have, even what he thinks he has will be taken from him."[b] Without the Essene perspective, these sayings seem unfair. Jesus presented a veiled teaching; he did not reveal all of his knowledge. Those who were interested by this first message could follow him and become one of his disciples.[25] During the time of Jesus, the Essenes believed that the last days were upon them and they poured forth to preach their message about the kingdom of God. Jesus chose seventy-two followers and told them, "The harvest is plentiful, but the workers are few."[c]

It appears that Jesus used the Essenic method of exorcism when driving out demons, especially in the Gerasenes when he sent the legion of demons into the pigs. Jesus, like the Essenes, demanded that the leading demon tell his name. Knowing the name had magical significance and gave him control over the demons. Only selected early Christians were given this power. First Jesus gave the twelve disciples authority over evil spirits and sent them out. They drove out

---

[a] Mark 4:11.
[b] Luke 8:18.
[c] Luke 10:2.

many demons and healed many sick people.[a] In the book of Luke, Jesus sent out the seventy-two followers in the same way. When they returned they said, "Lord, even the demons submit to us *in your name*." Even after Jesus was killed, they continued to invoke the name of Jesus. Peter said, "In the name of Jesus Christ of Nazareth, walk."[b] We have become very used to this phraseology, so we never think about what was meant by it in the time right after Jesus was killed. Why would people say, "In the name of the preacher who was killed..."? They were claiming the authority that they believed the name conferred.

Essenes carried nothing with them as they traveled. The staff which members received symbolized their knowledge of the secret laws of life and the ability to use them harmoniously for cleansing and healing. Jesus charged the twelve disciples to "take nothing for the journey except a staff; no bread, no bag, no money in your belts; but to wear sandals and not put on two tunics."[c] Essenes also washed each other's feet, as a sign of friendship and to cultivate the idea that they must take care of each other as the Father of all took care of them. Jesus washed the feet of the twelve and told them to serve each other. By taking care of the individual, Essenes were taking care of the God who was behind him. Jesus said, "I was hungry and you gave me food, I was thirsty and you

---

[a] Mark 6:7
[b] Acts 3:6
[c] Mark 6:8

gave me drink, I was a stranger and you welcomed me, I was naked and you clothed me, I was sick and you visited me, I was in prison and you came to me...[A]s you did it to one of the least of these my brethren, you did it to me."[a]

The Essenes chose to live without goods and without property; Jesus chose to live without goods or property. The Essenes avoided wholesale and retail commerce, believing it led to covetousness. Jesus drove out those who were buying and selling in the temple. He overturned the tables of the moneychangers. The Essenes considered their Brotherhood as the presence on earth of the teaching of the sons of God. Is this what the writers of the New Testament meant when they referred to Jesus as the son of God? The Essenes were the light which shines in the darkness and which invites the darkness to change itself into light. Jesus said "I am the light of the world; he who follows me will not walk in darkness, but will have the light of life."[b]

The Essenes had a hierarchical structure. The highest Essene priest was known as Christos (Anointed One). Is this what Jesus meant when he answered the Jewish high priest that he was the Christ? The Essenes had a second position known as the Messiah who was to undergo and suffer physical abuse in atonement for the sins of the whole community, enduring scourging and vengeance on his body. This does not fit what happened to Jesus because he was flogged as a criminal and

---

[a] Matthew 25:36.
[b] John 8:12.

crucified as a blasphemer. The Essenes called themselves Therapeutae, "healers," claiming that their simple, moral lifestyle gave them the power to cast out demons of sickness and even to restore life to the dead. Considering this, Jesus raising Lazarus from the dead seems a typical Essenic miracle. Some have wondered if this is how Jesus was raised from the tomb following his crucifixion. Essenes might have come to the tomb to revive him.

All who joined the Essene sect gave away or sold their worldly goods and gave the profits to the sect's leaders. They deposited their salaries into the common fund for the use of all in the group. This would explain the hard teaching of Jesus to the rich young man. Jesus said, "If you want to enter life, obey the commandments...If you want to be perfect, go, sell your possessions and give to the poor, and you will have treasure in heaven. Then come, follow me."[a] In Acts we read that "All the believers were one in heart and mind. No one claimed that any of his possessions was his own, but they shared everything they had."[b] Whether some of the first communities were called Essenic or Christian the rules were strictly enforced. This is seen in the story of the husband and wife, Ananias and Sapphira, in the book of Acts. It was discovered that they had kept some of the proceeds of the sale of their property for themselves without telling the community. When Peter questioned the husband about this and accused him of lying to

[a] Matthew 19:17.
[b] 4:32

the Holy Spirit, the man fell down dead. Then Peter questioned the wife about this, and she also died when she heard what had happened to her husband. The local authorities later arrested Peter and some of the group for murder, but they miraculously escaped. (Acts 5:2-10,18-19)[26]

I don't know enough about the Essenes to declare that Jesus was a member, but it is an intriguing possibility and the similarities are almost too numerous to ignore. If Jesus was an Essene, either there were multiple branches or he had risen through the ranks high enough that he could make his own rules, because not all of his teachings match all of theirs. They strictly held the Sabbath; Jesus often healed on the Sabbath. They were strict vegetarians; Jesus sometimes ate fish and lamb. They had cleanliness rules and ritual washings and Jesus declared that these weren't necessary. They avoided oil on their skin; Jesus accepted the anointing at Bethany with expensive perfume. Some Essenes had unflattering views of women; Jesus included women in his ministry. Perhaps Jesus lived and studied with the Essenes for ten years before breaking off to start his own ministry. Perhaps during his 40 days in the wilderness he struggled with whether he would go back to the Essenes or reach out to others to bring them to a new way of life and relationship with God and others.

Release to the Captives

$\mathbf{M}$any people today survive; they exist – they don't live. They are trapped in lives that contain no joy, no satisfaction, no peace. I don't know why they get up in the morning or why they eat. Perhaps they live as animals who get up because the sun has come up and eat because they are hungry. More likely it is because of family responsibilities or just out of habit. This is not the way anyone needs to live; it is not the way anyone should live. When I try to define what could transform existence into life, I turn instinctively to the New Testament, but neither the synoptic gospels, James, or the book of Acts contain the traditional message of salvation, and I have rejected the message of the apostles John and Paul. Jesus did not just say, "Obey the God of the Old Testament." He showed us how to *live*. He showed us the kind of relationship we could have with God and how to live with our fellow human beings. He showed how right living could bring inner peace and joy. The God of the Old Testament was cold, distant, judgmental. Jesus brought him warmth, closeness, mercy. But Christianity, and especially the deification of Christ, risks limiting "God" to what fits in our God-shaped box. It limits God and makes him personal, but small. We lose our awe. We lose the sense of mystery. We lose the power. The ultimate meaning of religion is not that you get a best friend who will always accept you no matter what. Religion is about our relationship with things eternal, things beyond this world. It is about rising above our worst selves and nurturing our higher nature.

Many people are trapped in lives of quiet desperation. Jesus came to proclaim release to the captives, to set free those who are downtrodden. The demons of today have different names than the demons of 2000 years ago. You may be tormented by debt, by threatened or current unemployment, by a dead-end job, by lack of education, by a bad relationship, by loneliness, meaninglessness, or boredom. When Jesus said, "I am the way...and the life" he meant "I'll show you the way to life, just follow me." He offers living water so that we may never thirst again. In the 21st century, we don't have the person of Jesus to turn to. What we have are the principles, the blueprint, the roadmap showing us the path to abundant life.

The first key is that an abundant life does not come from an abundance of things; it comes from an abundance of love. Not love in the narrow romantic sense; love in the deep caring for others sense. Love for friends, love for strangers. Love for the God who created you and this wonderful world. A love that makes you want to do the right things, things that will help and please the people around you; things that will please your God. When you give love, you will be showered with love in return. Some of it will be subtle: a smile, a sincere thank you, a look of relief from someone who expected you to be angry even though they're doing their best. Trusting God with a simple "Thy will be done". God's guidance comes from many sources. The United States is a country with many resources. There are many programs to get you what you need whether it's education, protection from an abusive spouse, or financial counseling. Opportunities abound when you set your sights on serving others, and your needs will be met in the process. When you stop looking for what the world can give you and focus on what you can give the world, this is a wonderful place.

I reach out to all those who knew God in their childhood, but as they matured rejected the irrational tenets of their parents' faith. God does exist. God does care. Jesus did live and heal and preach. Don't let what others have added to what Jesus said and did drive you away from God and doing his work.

Living in the World

In his book *Loving God*, Charles Colson quotes Dick Halverson, "Nowhere in the Bible is the world exhorted to 'come to church.' But the church's mandate is clear: she must go to the world...the work of ministry belongs to the one in the pew, not the one in the pulpit." And Colson continues, "The church comes together on Sunday mornings principally to be prepared to carry out its ministry the rest of the week in every walk of life." And later "The isolated church keeps evangelizing the same people over and over until its only mission finally is to entertain itself." Ouch. One of the reasons I have always enjoyed going to church is the music. I have participated in church music programs since the third grade. It has never been enough for me to go to church on Sunday mornings, but I have supplemented that with Bible studies or choir practices, not my own ministry to the world. Like millions of Americans, I considered myself a good Christian because I went to church on a regular basis. Now the reality slaps me in the face. Jesus didn't say, "Go to church." He said, "Take care of my sheep."

Christian education for those who are young in the faith is a legitimate purpose of the organized church. And adults need some ongoing guidance to keep them on the right path. But that right path is *doing* the work of tending to God's people. Ninety percent of churches are content to tend only to the flocks within their own walls and not out in their communities. Jesus came to seek and save the lost. There is a saying that God has no hands but our hands; God has no voice but our voices. Are you using them to *do* the things that Jesus would have you do?

Our economy is hugely over-inflated. If people voluntarily dropped out of our economy, there could be a soft landing. If people adopted a simple lifestyle and resigned from high pressure, high-paying jobs, then people who had not yet adopted a simple lifestyle could take some of those jobs as overall demand decreased and they got laid off from other jobs. But those people who might leave high-paying jobs can't just go to zero income. Everyone needs to eat and needs a heated place to live. And we've created a society in which transportation isn't optional. Demand for those things wouldn't increase, so there wouldn't be more low-wage, low-pressure jobs. Perhaps some two-income families would decide it was better for one of them to quit working and take care of the home and community. Perhaps people would work fewer hours to spend time on things that are more important. That would open up jobs for people who had stepped out of higher pressure, higher-paying jobs. And perhaps as people began to spend more time with their families, demand for family-friendly activities would increase, opening up more jobs in those areas. As a child, I could never understand unemployment. In my mind, saying there were no jobs was the same as saying the world was perfect. There is always work to be done.

A full-time, salaried position used to mean forty hours of work per week. In some companies, it is now something more like indentured servitude. Many companies feel like they can make any demands of their salaried employees' time. Many salaried employees feel like they have to do whatever it takes. Maybe it's fifty hours a week. OK, sometimes it's sixty. And OK, sometimes you do a little bit of work on the weekend. What used to be a forty-hour-per-week job now consumes all of your waking hours. The whole premise of full-time work denies people the flexibility to adapt their work to their lifestyle. If someone would be happier working thirty hours a week and drawing seventy five percent of their salary and contributing toward their benefits, why should an employer say, "No, work 40 hours a week or quit"?

Jesus said he would pay those who were hired at the last hour the same as those who had worked all day, so the rewards will be the same for those who follow him all their lives and those who join him near the end of their lives. But he also said that whenever he comes only those who are prepared will go with him. How long you have followed him isn't the issue. This is not a decision that can be delayed. There is no later plane or train to catch. There will be no final boarding call. It is impossible to live an abundant life if you delay the decision until you have no life of any sort left to live.

To hear the words of Jesus and to put them into practice is to build yourself a strong foundation that will not wash away in a flood. Those who hear the words of Jesus, but listen to Paul that all they need to do is believe, will be washed away the moment a torrent strikes them. Jesus said "My mother and brothers are those who hear God's word *and put it into practice.*" "Lord, when did we see you hungry and feed you, or thirsty and give you something to drink? When did we see you a stranger and invite you in, or needing clothes and clothe you? When did we see you sick or in prison and go to visit you?" There are hungry people and people needing clothes in your town. For most of us, everyone is a stranger, because we don't invite anyone in. There are sick people and prisoners in your city. Have you done anything for the least of these brothers of the Lord?

Jesus said the most important commandment is "Love the Lord your God with all your heart and with all your soul and with all your mind and with all your strength." And "Love your neighbor as yourself." He said, "Do not store up for yourselves treasures on earth, where moth and rust destroy, and where thieves break in and steal. But store up for yourselves treasures in heaven." He didn't say, "If you've made your cash and non-cash donations for the year you've done your part." He said, "Do to others what you would have them do to you." Jesus' ministry was all about living here in this world. He taught us about relationship with God and relationship with our fellow humans. He taught us where our priorities should be.

It "is not just a matter of Jesus' words or even faith in Jesus' words; rather, it is a matter of accepting Jesus' lifestyle, following Jesus' program, and thereby living within the radicality of God's kingdom here and now."[27]

Spiritual Discipline

Jesus discussed fasting in all three of the synoptic gospels. Jesus fasted for forty days prior to beginning his ministry. During his ministry, neither Jesus or his disciples fasted, but he said the guests of the bridegroom (the disciples) would fast when the bridegroom was taken from them. He said *when you* fast, fix your hair (my modern interpretation) and wash your face so that it will not be obvious to others that you are fasting. He said that fasting increased the effectiveness of prayer in bringing about healing. After his crucifixion it is not clear that the disciples did fast, but at least the prophets and teachers at Antioch, including Barnabas and Saul did. Fasting has been part of many religions for centuries as a way to demonstrate the earnestness of the one fasting and as a way to withdraw from the physical world and draw closer to the spiritual world. This has been carried forward as part of some modern religions. Jews practice fasting on Yom Kippur as a sign of atonement. Muslims practice fasting during the month of Ramadan as a way to draw closer to God. The Qur'an says, "Fasting is prescribed to you as it was prescribed to those before you, that you may (learn) self-restraint."[a]

The practice of fasting has evolved within the Orthodox, Roman Catholic, and Protestant churches. The Lenten fast went from a forty hour fast to a forty day fast with one meal allowed each day in the sixth century. Officially, there are now two fasting days, Ash Wednesday and Good Friday. In practice, fasting has gone through many strange variations. Many Catholics abstained from red meat and poultry one day a week. Some Protestants give up one item of food or drink such as chocolate, potato chips, or Coke during Lent. These variations do not capture the essence of fasting. They demonstrate what small sacrifices most modern Christians are willing to make for their religion. I'm not willing to give up a source of animal protein, let alone skip a meal, but I'll substitute fish for a land animal. I'm not willing to give up between meal snacks for a few weeks, let alone skip a meal, but I'll substitute different snacks. Over the years, fasting has drawn criticism for false piety and for aggravation of some medical conditions, and there is no specific call for

---

[a] Surah 2 verse 183

fasting in the New Testament. However, I suspect that one of the main reasons that total abstinence from food for any period of time has fallen from favor is that few modern Western Christians have the discipline to make it through the specified period without giving in to the desire of the body for food. While other cultures routinely fast as a spiritual discipline, our culture does not value spiritual discipline. Many Americans are not willing to deny their physical desires for health or moral reasons, either.

Earthly Parents

Jesus seems to have had mixed feelings about earthly parents. He more than once picked out "Honor your mother and father" as one of the greatest commandments. But when his mother and brothers came to speak to him, he said of his disciples "Here are my mother and my brothers", and later "do not call anyone on earth 'father' for you have one Father, and he is in heaven." It is as if the discovery of his heavenly father negated any need for an earthly father. It seems that his message was "Don't disrespect your parents, but other things are more important". It is odd that the last we hear of Joseph, Jesus' father, was when Jesus was twelve years old, when he was found in "his Father's house." Jesus' official recognition as an adult would have been shortly after this. It is clear from how Jesus turned out that Joseph must have done a good job raising him for the first twelve years of his life. There is no mention of Joseph dying, but his mother is mentioned right up to the end of the gospels, and at the end, it is suggested that she is a widow. Jesus' earthly parents were not his priority, but he did make provision for his mother at his death. Stephen Mitchell, in his book *The Gospel According to Jesus* (and his sources), take the phrase "Jesus son of Mary" in Mark as having a derogatory sense of illegitimacy. However, if Joseph died shortly after the incident at the temple in Jerusalem when Jesus was 12, wouldn't Jesus son of Mary be the common way to refer to him?

So many of this country's problems are caused by the lack of an earthly father. Single motherhood can lead to the kind of poverty that Jesus associated with widowhood. In Jesus' day, a widow without a son had no means of support. In 1997, less than two thirds of never-married mothers ever finished high school which leaves them with no means of support. Having only one parent in the house is the surest indicator that a family will have a low income and other problems. In 1997, sixty-nine percent of children living with just their never married mother were near or below the poverty line.[28] Earthly fathers are needed to provide moral guidance and financial stability for at least the first thirteen years of a child's life.

It is amazing to me that a mother would *choose* to work full-time and entrust the majority of her pre-school-age child's (or children's) waking hours to someone else (other than their father). Americans rate care by a child's own mother as the single most desirable type of care for children. Yet that's not the option that the majority of American families choose. According to the Bureau of Labor Statistics, 54 percent of married mothers with infants under age one work outside the home, and 61 percent of all children under 3 now have mothers who work. More married mothers are working to increase the family's income. Of the 20 percent of families earning the highest income, more than one-half had two earners with full-time jobs. [29] And the number of families making more than $50,000 has increased to 32% of the population.[30] These women aren't working because they need the income to afford basic housing, food, or clothing. Raising children is not a job like cleaning the house to be put off on someone else whose time is not as valuable as your own. There is no way to separate the feeding and general care of a child from the imparting of moral values and the sense of what is important in life. The child will pick up these things from the people they are around for the majority of their waking hours. And a message from the parents comes through loud and clear: It's more important for us to spend time earning money than spending it with family, community, or friends.

I have no problem with mothers of young children working a few hours a day or week for whatever reason. That is the choice I made with my children both because I needed to escape from the 24/7 demands of raising children and to exercise my mind. But I never worked so many hours that I relinquished the position of primary caregiver of my preschool-age children, and once they were in school full-time I was at least still in competition with their teachers for spending the most waking time with them. Among families with the highest 20 percent of income, 11 percent had four or more workers. Families with incomes over $50,000 have an average of 2.2 workers.[31] I interpret this to mean that by the time children of two-income families reach the age of sixteen they have internalized the message that the goal of life is to earn income. There is nothing wrong with teenagers working part time. It is a productive use of their time that keeps them from destructive uses of their time. But I question the motivation for why these kids are choosing to spend their time earning money, not building relationships with family and friends or working with the community.

When there is no father in the house (either because the parents were never married or through divorce or death) a mother faces the choices of having someone else raising her child (or children) or no income. Not surprisingly, any woman with the potential to earn more than the cost of childcare normally chooses that option. And with high quality childcare the children are usually fine. Problems arise when the mother doesn't have the potential to earn more than the cost of childcare. Fifty-nine percent of never-married moms were not employed in 1997. With no income, suddenly society is left with the tab to raise these children and their mothers. And society probably wouldn't mind if those women raised responsible children who grew into productive members of society (which some do), but it tends to be a self-perpetuating problem with many children of poor single mothers growing up to themselves become poor single parents. Why? Many of these mothers are young and uneducated and haven't yet learned to be responsible themselves, so they cannot convey to their children the importance of being responsible. The largest group of children who live with just their mothers have divorced mothers in their thirties. The next largest group have mothers in their twenties who have never married and a significant number are even younger. [32] How can this cycle be broken?

Because government is part of the problem, government has to be part of the solution. The government should never subsidize housing and food with no strings attached because that gives neither the means or the incentive to break the cycle. Assistance should be tied to the mother's age and education level, for example, a sixteen year old mother could be given two years of food *and childcare* assistance so she can get her high school diploma or equivalency. She shouldn't need housing assistance because she should still be living with her parents. Eighteen to twenty-five year old mothers could be given one year of housing, food, childcare, and training assistance so they could complete a GED or vocational training. Ideally, the plans would be tailored to the individual's situation. This plan would be more expensive in the short term, but the benefits to society should be immediate, and in the long term, it should be less expensive than the current policy of subsidizing life. The objective of assistance to women and children should be to move them from the category of not being able to earn more than the cost of childcare to being able to support themselves and their children. This is the equivalent of restoring life to the son so the mother is not left without means of support.

In the private sector, there are missions for rescuing those who have fallen through the cracks of the government system. The best homeless shelters provide not only food and shelter for the short-term, but addiction programs, education and job training, family training, childcare, and spiritual guidance to restore wholeness to lives that are broken. These shelters often employ some of their own temporary residents or graduates. These shelters deserve whatever support we can give them. They follow Jesus' example of reaching out to the lowest strata of society and restoring them to community. They in turn provide an example for communities that do not have a comprehensive rescue mission and for government agencies charged with serving this same clientele.

So government and private agencies can play a role in alleviating the problems of low-income single mothers. Individuals can also play a role, working with these or other agencies or independent of them, educating the mothers or the children, providing childcare, assisting with food. Jesus advocated a society where the poor were so morally upright that those who had some means would have no qualms about taking them into their houses and directly providing food and shelter. We have a lot of work to do for that to be generally true now.

Jesus, God, Us

Jesus told many parables in which the master (God) is away on a journey. Does this mean that God is not actively involved in our world? Western Christians believe in a highly personal God, praying for recovery from a cold or to do well on a test. They have trouble reconciling that God is all-powerful and all-knowing with the fact that bad things happen. Karen Armstrong, in her excellent *History of God*, says this comes from an anthropomorphic conception of God. I think it comes from not taking our "Father" image of God far enough. There are over 6 billion people on this planet. It's not that God *couldn't* listen and respond to all those prayers; I don't believe he cares about that kind of detail. I believe He cares about big things like rulers of countries and big wars. To believe that God cares about every tiny detail of our lives belittles God and sets us up for disillusionment when all of those requests are not granted. Christians say if a prayer isn't granted, it wasn't in God's will, but how do you explain it when the bad guy lives and the good guy dies? Our God is a big god. You don't call the president of the United States when a street light goes out on your street. It's up to us to handle the details of our lives. It's up to us to look after our neighbors and to rely on our neighbors when we are in need.

Many have asked, "Where was God during the holocaust?" "The holocaust challenged the notion that God is both all-good and all-powerful. If God was all-good, then God could not be all-powerful because God did not intervene to stop the slaughter of innocent men, women, and children."[33] God intervenes in human history through humans, not directly. The holocaust recalls the biblical story of Esther. It was proposed to King Xerxes: "There is a certain people dispersed and scattered among the peoples in all the provinces of your kingdom whose customs are different from those of other people and who do not obey the king's laws; it is not in the king's best interest to tolerate them. If it pleases the king, let a decree be issued to destroy them, and I will put ten thousand talents of silver into the royal treasury for the men who carry out this business."

The King's seal was given to this decree and "Dispatches were sent by couriers to all the king's provinces with the orders to destroy, kill and annihilate all the Jews – young and old, women and little children – on a single day... and to plunder their goods." Prior to this, King Xerxes' queen had been deposed and replaced by Esther, a Jewess who had kept her background and nationality a secret. Esther was afraid to approach the king about this edict because it carried a high probability of her death and a low probability of success. But her cousin Mordecai persuaded her with the words "who knows but that you have come to royal position for such a time as this." Esther fasted and asked all of the Jews of her citadel to fast for her. She plied the king with banquets and then made her request to grant her life and to spare her people. The edict sealed with the king's ring could not be revoked, but he issued a new edict granting the Jews "the right to assemble and protect themselves; to destroy, kill, and annihilate any armed force of any nationality or province that might attack them." When this edict was declared, "many people of other nationalities became Jews because fear of the Jews had seized them." On the appointed day "no one could stand against [the Jews] because the people of all of the other nationalities were afraid of them." In the days that followed the Jews killed 75,800 of their enemies.

Not exactly a Christian storybook ending to the story, however it provides a telling example as to how God intervenes in history. God allowed the right person to be in the right place at the right time. That person responded by summoning all the spiritual resources she had at her disposal and making a high risk decision. A different person in a different time and place – say Germany in the 1930s and '40s – may have reacted in a different manner, deciding to remain silent. Do I think God had selected one specific person who was in a position that he or she could have prevented the holocaust? It's possible. God is not known for operating through committees. He is a God of personal responsibility. The Bible is a book of individuals who made a difference in the history of God's people. The notion of an all-powerful God conjures up images of a divine puppeteer. God is not a puppeteer. He is a father of millions of children. He provides them with guidance. He provides them with opportunity. But they operate under their own free will.

Does the outcome of the holocaust deny the basic sovereignty of God? God is not a God of numbers. He is not like the rulers of this world who measure their power by the

number of their subjects. God's "human experiment" once got
so out of hand that he erased the slate and started over. But he
then promised he would never again destroy the whole world
by flood. God is a God of epochs. The first epoch ended with
Noah's flood. Thousands of years passed. Many of even the
"righteous" were not living the way God wanted them to live.
So he prompted Jesus to begin a public ministry. Indirectly,
that ministry changed the way that millions of people live, and
the way that millions of people died. The holocaust was part of
that epoch. Perhaps God is deciding that it is again time to
intervene in history in a major way, and he will work through a
Jew, a Muslim, or a Christian or through one of the other
millions of possibilities he has on earth to redirect the path of
history. "In the Bible and so many other religious texts, God is
pictured as fire...Fire is not an object. Fire is a process of
releasing the energy concealed in a lump of coal or a piece of
wood. That is what God does. He releases the energy hidden
in every one of us...The death of a good person diminishes
God's presence on earth."[34]

It is both common sense and a part of many religious
traditions that we become more like what our minds dwell on.
Many traditions contain standard prayers that by repetition
become part of the fiber of the individuals who pray them. I
sometimes use a mantra, a short phrase repeated over and over
again with intentional breathing to reinforce who I want to be.
One of my favorites is, "God is present through me." I picture
those incubator gloves by which a person on the outside can
handle a vulnerable infant inside without risk of introducing

germs. What actually touches the infant is the gloves, but what moves them is the person on the outside of the incubator. In the same way, I try to make my hands and the rest of me available for God's use, so He can touch others through me.

Naturalism, Literalism

There are some who, in looking for truth in the New Testament, discount the miracles of Jesus as embellishments, added by those trying to justify the divinity of Jesus. But, if you remove the virgin birth, remove the miracles, and remove the resurrection (for those who are going to discount miracles are not going to acknowledge virgin births or rising from the dead), what is left? A preacher. Perhaps a very good one, but I'm sure around that time there were other good preachers, and since then there have been thousands. There is nothing in the words of Jesus that would have attracted the kind of attention that Jesus attracted, nothing that would have started a new religion. The miracles had to have happened or none of it makes sense. In the books of Mark and Luke, Jesus drives out an evil spirit, heals many including a leper and a paralytic, and crowds followed him, before any preaching is mentioned. In Matthew's account, Jesus announced his ministry by quoting Isaiah and began to preach, "Repent, for the kingdom of heaven is near." Jesus went throughout Galilee healing every disease and sickness and large crowds from Galilee and all the surrounding regions followed him. Try to attract a crowd anywhere in any century by preaching, "Repent, for the kingdom of heaven is near." Jesus used his healing power to attract attention.

In his book *The Birth of Christianity*, John D. Crossan states that everyone has presuppositions about the gospels. He lists some possible choices. First, the gospel authors could be like four witnesses giving legal testimony. Many Christians and Christian authors use this presupposition. Second, the gospel authors could be like four historians conducting oral interviews. I believe Mark falls into this category. Third, the gospel authors could be like four scholars doing basic research. I believe Luke falls into this category. Fourth, the gospel authors could be like four evangelists rewriting earlier tradition. I believe both Matthew and John fall into this category. Crossan puts all four in this category. William L. Craig uses the first presupposition in his book *Will the Real Jesus Please Stand Up?* I would like to comment on four "facts" Craig includes in his book.

As fact 1, he lists "After his crucifixion Jesus was buried by Joseph of Arimathea in his personal tomb." As his third piece of evidence for this fact, he states that "as a member of the Jewish court that condemned Jesus, Joseph of Arimathea is unlikely to be a Christian invention." In the book of Mark, Joseph of Arimathea is described as "a prominent member of the council, who was himself waiting for the kingdom of God." In Matthew's account it says, "who had himself become a disciple of Jesus." Luke says he had not consented to the council's plan and actions. I don't think many people accuse Joseph of Arimathea of being a Christian invention, but some might accuse him of being a Christian sympathizer with incentive to hide the body or deliver him to Essene healers.

As fact 2, Craig states "On the Sunday following the crucifixion, the tomb of Jesus was found empty by a group of his women followers." In my opinion, he skipped over a couple of important facts to get to this one.

1-- Pilate was surprised to hear that Jesus was already dead. Crucifixion was usually a long, agonizing death. The other two crucified with Jesus were still alive on the day of preparation. Only in John's gospel do we find the story about one of the soldiers piercing Jesus' side with a spear and blood and water coming out. In Mark's account, Pilate simply asked the centurion, who said he was dead. In Matthew's and Luke's telling there is no question and no confirmation that he is dead. Joseph of Arimathea simply takes the body.

2 -- According to Matthew, on the evening of the same day that Jesus was hung on the cross, Joseph took Jesus' body, and he personally rolled a large stone against the entrance of the tomb and went away. Mary Magdalene and the other Mary were sitting opposite the grave. Mark and Luke report that Mary Magdalene and Mary the mother of Joses (or the women) saw him laid in the tomb. Matthew continues with "the next day ... the stone was sealed and a guard posted." Luke continues his telling on the Sabbath (the following day). Mark picks up the story "when the Sabbath was over." Could the two women have rolled away the stone that Joseph of Arimathea rolled against the entrance of the tomb? Could they have removed the body? Could they have reported back to the

disciples who certainly could have rolled away the stone and removed the body? Might they have delivered it to Peter or another healer? In Acts 9:40, Peter raised Dorcus from the dead. Why not Jesus? Matthew himself reports that the story that his disciples stole Jesus away was widely circulated. Now we are ready for Craig's Fact #2. "On the Sunday following the crucifixion, the tomb of Jesus was found empty."

Resurrection

In his response entitled "The Irrelevancy of the Empty Tomb" Marcus Borg makes an intriguing distinction between resuscitation and resurrection. He states that when someone is resuscitated, their physical body returns to the life they had before and will die again someday. Jesus resuscitated Jairus' daughter. He resuscitated Lazarus. After Jesus died, he did not return to the life he led before. In Jesus' day, "the resurrection" was understood to be an age when *all* who were considered worthy would be raised from the dead into a new kind of existence in spiritual bodies. The resurrected Jesus was considered to be the "first fruits" of the resurrection. As more time passed, the writers of the New Testament were forced to come up with new explanations of the resurrection, resorting to referring to "those who have fallen asleep." "We believe that Jesus died and rose again and so we believe that God will bring with Jesus those who have fallen asleep in him... [W]e who are still alive...will certainly not precede those who have fallen asleep... [T]he dead in Christ will rise first."[a] So Jesus really didn't fit the first century expectation of resurrection.

As fact 3 in his book, Craig states "On multiple occasions and under various circumstances different individuals and groups of people experienced appearances of Jesus alive from the dead." Borrowing Borg's language, Craig believes that Jesus' body was resuscitated, but he didn't resume his earthly ministry and he didn't assume an earthly kingship. Did he move away from the spotlight and the hounding of the crowds to have a normal life? The original ending of the oldest gospel of Mark contains no resurrection appearances. In the next oldest gospel of Matthew, Jesus appears to Mary Magdalene and the other Mary and to the eleven disciples (Judas had committed suicide) and speaks a total of 5 sentences. In Luke's gospel Jesus appeared to the eleven disciples and those with them, spoke to them, ate with them, then left them and was taken up into heaven. In Luke's second book (Acts) he says that Jesus appeared to "these men" over a period of forty days.

In John's gospel, Jesus appears to Mary Magdalene, to ten disciples, to eleven disciples, then to seven disciples in the story of the miraculous catch of fish, which Luke places at the beginning of Jesus' ministry when he was very much alive. The risen Jesus invited Thomas to touch him. John's gospel doesn't specifically say that Thomas did touch him, but makes

---

[a] 1 Thessalonians 4:14.

it clear that he could have. In 1 Corinthians, Paul says Jesus appeared to Peter, then to the twelve (twelve?) then to more than 500 of the brothers at the same time, then to James, then to all the apostles, then to him. These appearances match none of the gospels or the book of Acts, and Paul was not a witness. In each retelling of the story, there are more appearances to more people, over a longer period, more words are spoken, food is introduced, and physical contact is implied.

In John, Jesus said "before long, the world will not see me any more, but you will see me…On that day you will realize that I am in my Father, and you are in me, and I am in you…He who loves me will be loved by my Father, and I too will love him and show myself to him."[a] In many of the resurrection accounts, the witnesses don't even recognize Jesus at first. He is recognized when they are called by name or by performing a characteristic gesture. First century Jews had no basis, no language for the continuing presence of Jesus without the language of resurrection. Is it possible that Jesus' closest friends and disciples began to experience Christ in other people around them, but as the stories spread, they spread as stories of the physical return of Jesus?

In 1764 François-Marie de Voltaire defined ideal religion in his *Philosophical Dictionary* as "that which taught much morality and very little dogma? That which tended to make men just without making them absurd? That which did

---

[a] 14:19

not order one to believe in things that are impossible, contradictory, injurious to divinity, and pernicious to mankind, and which dared not menace with eternal punishment anyone possessing common sense?" At the end of his ministry, Jesus was executed by the government. In Matthew's gospel, at his death, Jesus cried out "My God, My God, why have you forsaken me?" This is the cry of one for whom things are not turning out as he had planned. And Paul would have us eternally condemned unless we accept his story that Jesus laid down his life willingly as payment for our sins.

Today many Christians put Jesus in a category by himself. Jesus was resurrected; Christians "go to heaven" when they die. Scriptural support for this is extremely thin. In Matthew, Jesus makes the vague statement "Rejoice and be glad, because great is your reward in heaven..."[a] The best evidence may be Jesus' words in Luke, "the time came when the beggar died and the angels carried him to Abraham's side"[b] and "today you will be with me in paradise."[c] One verse that is often quoted in support of this view is "In my Father's house are many rooms; if it were not so would I have told you that I go to prepare a place for you?" But he continues "And when I go and prepare a place for you, I will come again and will take you to myself, that where I am you may be also."[d] I do not

---

[a] 5:12
[b] 16:22
[c] Luke 23:43
[d] John 14:02

take this statement to mean that Jesus is an innkeeper, going to fluff pillows in one room, then coming back to retrieve one follower, then going to fluff pillows in the next room, then coming back to retrieve the next one from his deathbed. I read it to mean that Jesus would be coming back within that first generation and taking all of his followers "to himself". This hasn't happened yet.

The Bible provides very little support for the idea that each believer "goes to heaven" when he dies. It is actually easier to disprove this individual transport to heaven by quoting the Bible than to support it. In Matthew, Jesus says, "For the Son of Man *is going to come* in his Father's glory with his angels, and *then* he will reward each person according to what he has done."[a] In John, he says, "No one has ever gone into heaven except the one who came from heaven."[b] Later he is even more explicit. Jesus said, "Now is the time for judgment on this world; now the prince of this world will be driven out. But I, when I am lifted up from the earth, will draw all men to myself."[c] He was saying, "The judgment is now and when I ascend (after the first Easter) I'll take people with me." In Acts, Peter says, "David did not ascend to heaven."[d] In his first letter to the Thessalonians Paul says, "For the Lord himself will come down from heaven, with a loud command,

---

[a] 16:27
[b] 3:13
[c] John 12:31
[d] 2:34

with the voice of the archangel and with the trumpet call of God, and the dead in Christ will rise first."[a]

So we are left with the Old Testament concept of Sheol, the Greek Hades, or the Catholic concept of purgatory to serve as a warehouse for all of the souls of those who have "fallen asleep" until the return of Christ. Why do so many people believe in the immortality of the soul? Because we want to. Plato said, "all men will necessarily desire immortality". We need to know there's more to life than this. This life's not fair, and in the end we want it to be fair.

And what of Satan?

Demons and Satan are significant characters in the New Testament, but rarely mentioned in the Old Testament. Neither Jesus or Paul introduces them as new concepts; they are accepted as already known. Where did they come from? In early Hebrew belief, all history was the result of two forces: God and human will. In the Old Testament (primarily in the book of Job), Satan was the accuser, sort of a prosecuting attorney within God's circle. The few times that the word "demons" is used in the Old Testament it refers to foreign, powerless gods. The word devil is never used in the Old Testament. In the Old Testament, Hebrews believed that the soul went to Sheol to abide for a brief period after death before

---

[a] 4:16

fading completely from existence. Judaism was primarily a this-world religion. The only evil spirit in the Old Testament is the one that plagued King Saul, the one that David assuaged by playing his harp. By contrast, in the earliest gospels, one of Jesus' primary activities was driving out evil spirits. And Satan plays a minor but pivotal role. How did this happen?

The Israelites of the Old Testament managed to live apart, usually physically, from foreign influences. When they entered Canaan, they destroyed all of the previous inhabitants; for the next 750 years, they lived in relative isolation from other religions. During the Assyrian reign, we only hear from prophets, and from them we hear that this was a period of moral and religious decline. When the Hebrews were sent into exile in Babylon, we hear of the behavior of the exemplary Hebrews Daniel, Shadrach, Meshach, and Abednego. From the prophets we hear of continued moral and religious decline. So we have hundreds of years before the New Testament with Hebrews living side-by-side with Assyrians, Babylonians, and Greeks.

Going outside the Bible to historical sources, we find that during the Babylonian exile Persian elements were added to the Hebrew religion. The Hebrews gradually adopted the Persian idea that the universe is composed of two diametrically opposed forces, one good, the other evil. They also added belief in a dualistic afterlife: that the souls of the good would reunite with the principle of good in eternal bliss; the souls of the evil would reunite with the principle evil to suffer.[35] This is what caused the split between the Pharisees and the

Sadducees of Jesus' time. The Sadducees never accepted these Persian elements into the Hebrew religion. The Pharisees, however, added the beliefs in angels, demons, and eternal life of the soul.

Over hundreds of years, common people just absorbed these into their belief system -- that the world contained evil spirits, that their souls would go to eternal bliss or punishment. By the time Jesus began his ministry, talk of Satan, judgment, salvation, and heaven were not new concepts; they were familiar. Jesus did nothing to debunk these beliefs. On the contrary, he lent them credibility and further refined them. The writers of our New Testament speak as matter-of-factly about evil spirits as we would speak of the flu. They give no justification of their existence because they expected no questions or objections from their first century readers.

Whether we believe in them or not, Western minds tend to think of evil spirits as little beings. The King James version of the Bible uses the most literal translation of the Greek word now most commonly translated "evil" and that is "unclean". The Greek word pneuma, almost universally translated as "spirit" also means "breath". Using this translation, Jesus commanded the unclean breath to come out of a person as an initial step in healing. The New Testament is not explicit about Jesus replacing the unclean breath with the Breath of Life which is spoken of in the Old Testament[a], but this would fit

---

[a]Genesis 2:7 and others

with other ancient Asian healing processes. Maybe Jesus didn't believe in "evil spirits" any more than most people today. Perhaps it's more a problem of translation and modern understanding. Perhaps Jesus was simply commanding the "spirit of uncleanness" (the Chinese would call it the diseased chi) to come out of the person.

The second century Christian Justin "demoted the gods of Greco-Roman paganism to the status of demons. Instead of dismissing the existence of pagan gods, Justin maintained that they were real and powerful forces in the universe, but they were forces of evil..."[36] This has been the strategy of the Christian church ever since – any power not of God or Jesus is said to be of the Devil.

Today belief in evil spirits has been relegated to the fringe, whereas belief in the immortality of the soul is so widespread that proponents attribute this belief beyond themselves to groups that do not claim it as their own. Some of what was attributed to evil spirits in the Bible has been diagnosed as physical ailments or chemical imbalances in the brain. Some of what is called evil is simply the absence of moral guidance. Some of what is called evil is someone else's definition of good. This was the purpose of The Law: that within a society, all would share a definition of good and agree on punishment for those who strayed outside of what was good. Each society had its own Law. When one Law came into conflict with another Law there was War. The victors imposed their Law on the vanquished. Today we have societies living side by side with each other, interacting with each other, moving among each other. But not all those societies share a common definition of good.

Several steps back from September 11

We recently commemorated the fifth anniversary of September 11, 2001. With five years' perspective, we still struggle to understand what happened. How could people do this to other people? How could God let this happen? How could religious people think they were doing something that was in their god's will? Let us take another step back, maybe two. Much of the Muslim Middle East hates the United States of America for a couple of reasons. #1. Our arrogance: that we think we can go wherever we want and impose our will or manipulate other people to get what we want because we think we're right. #2. Our lifestyles and the values we promote, not just within our own society, but which we also try to export into theirs: consumerism, greed, exploitation of women, foul language. Which side of this are we on?

All of the individuals affected take it so personally. "My husband was a good person. Why would anyone kill him? Why would God let him be killed?" Let's start with the easier question: Why would anyone kill him? Because he worked or lived at the symbolic epicenter of a monster that is not content to dine on its own children, but lusts after growth that demands it seek out new sources to feed its insatiable appetite. Imagine you are a devout Muslim, living in the Middle East, trying to live a life that is pleasing to your God. But every day, new influences come and tempt your family to stray away from living a life that is pleasing to God. These temptations are not coming from within your own country. They are not coming from some ethereal devil. They are coming from the capitalists in the United States of America. So every day you struggle to live a good life against a growing tide that pulls your family away. Then one day a leader emerges, a *religious* leader, who says, "We must strike back against this great Satan before he destroys our country and our way of life." You might not follow this leader because you have family responsibilities and personal beliefs against what "striking back" would entail. But now imagine you are 20 years old. You have no family responsibilities; your responsibilities are to your God and your country. You must act before it's too late to save what your country stands for.

Do I approve of the methods of terror? Of course not. But I think Americans would do well to take it as a wake up call and not to sit around saying "poor me" and calling on the government to protect us from further attacks.

Do I think capitalism in itself is bed? No. Compare the first 200 years of capitalism in this country with the 60-year experiment in communism in other countries. The ideal of communism could never be realized in practice. Capitalism created good things until the emergence of multi-billion dollar corporations. These corporations are owned by shareholders who demand growth of their capital. Many of these corporations are in mature industries where all of the natural demand has already been met. To grow further they adopt marketing practices that stimulate excessive demand in this country, and try to get other countries to adopt our lust after things. In 2000, fifty-one of the world's largest one hundred economies were corporations, not countries. The top 500 corporations controlled forty-two percent of the *world's* wealth.[37] We need to examine the practices and policies that offend Muslim nations and find ways to contain them within our society, not force them on other societies.

Let's address the second question: Why would God let him be killed? Let's start in the book of Genesis. "God saw how corrupt the earth had become, for all the people on earth had corrupted their ways. So God said to Noah, 'I am going to put an end to all people, for the earth is filled with violence because of them.'"[a] We don't know what the population of the earth was at that time, but I bet it was more than the 3000 who were killed on September 11. And I bet that among the population Noah, his sons, and their wives were not the only good people. Society had become corrupt, and God decided the most expedient way to deal with it was to start over. Advantages of God's plan over terrorists: no injuries, no grieving family members, no shell-shocked fellow citizens.

Fast forward 1000 years. The LORD said, "The outcry against Sodom and Gomorrah is so great and their sin so grievous that I will go down and see if what they have done is

---

[a] 6:12

as bad as the outcry that has reached me."[a] Then Abraham begins to question the LORD. "Will you sweep away the righteous with the wicked? What if there are fifty righteous people in the city? Will you really sweep it away and not spare the place for the sake of the fifty righteous people in it?" And the LORD answers, "If I find fifty righteous people in the city of Sodom, I will spare the whole place for their sake." At this point Abraham tries to find the break point: forty-five, forty, thirty, twenty, ten. "For the sake of ten, I will not destroy it." As it turned out God could only find six righteous people, but three of them wouldn't listen or follow instructions, so the other three were saved and he destroyed those cities, their inhabitants, and all the vegetation on the surrounding plain. Again, no injuries, unless you count being turned into a pillar of salt. This time, however, Lot lost his wife and his daughters lost their fiancés.

Jesus called for reform one individual at a time, trying to save Israel from corruption. The radical Muslims of the Middle East are going for something more akin to the Old Testament population purges to eliminate the problem. If God had decided to deal with the problem of American corruption and sin directly, would he have targeted the World Trade Towers? Probably not, but if we can use ancient history as a guide, he might have taken out the entire city of New York and

---

[a] Genesis 18:20

its suburbs after removing a few people. If we look to the book of Revelation, he still might.

Life and Death

In the United States, so much of what we call life is concerned with death. We have wars against aspects of death: A war on cancer, a war on heart disease, eternal preparation for wars against political foes. Death – the great enemy which must be overcome so that we can get into life which has no death.[38] Instead of living, we try to kill death. What would we do if on the 6:00 news tonight it was announced that simple, inexpensive cures for asthma, diabetes, AIDS, cancers, heart disease, lung diseases, etc. had been found? And ironclad treaties had been signed with all our enemies. What would we do? Is it possible that the reason Jesus cured lepers, paralytics, the blind, the deaf, and those with fevers and evil spirits, was to remove those distractions from the people so they could focus on what was important? Jesus raised a widow's son from the dead. If he had died, that would have left the widow without means of support. Did he raise the son to save the widow from poverty so that she could focus on something other than subsistence?

At the dawn of the 21st century Americans value life for its own sake. If some Americans had their way, every person that was ever conceived would live to the age of 100. All causes of death would be eliminated. The Qur'an says, "They will never seek for death, on account of the (sins) which their hands have sent on before them... You will find them, of all people, most greedy of life...each one of them wishes he could be given a life of a thousand years."[a] Seemingly, many Americans place very little value on quality of life, either physical or spiritual. Children born with horrible defects undergo millions of dollars worth of surgeries. People whose quality of life has been totally and permanently ravaged by disease or injury still have the quantity of their days extended by millions of dollars worth of drugs, surgery, and mechanical devices. In many cases, not only the individuals' lives, but also those of their families are totally consumed by their health concerns. This is not God's way. Jesus healed many. *Healed* them. One touch and they were whole, restored. The only cost was their faith. In many cases, he removed their dependence on society. He came that we might have life, *and have it abundantly.*

Medical technology has given us the means to extend the lives of those born with severe defects or afflicted by lifelong diseases or injuries. Our Judeo-Christian heritage gives us very little guidance on whether we *should* extend those lives. For lack of more specific guidance, many cling desperately to "Thou shalt not kill" which was always a poor translation. The commandment is "You shall not murder". It does not say you must provide whatever medical intervention is required to prevent death. Origen, a Christian who lived in the third century AD held that "death was not to be

---

[a] Surah 2 verses 95-96

feared...because it was the final liberation of the soul from the body."[39] When a pet, farm animal, or race horse is severely injured, most people do not question that the animal should be "put out of its misery" rather than allowing it to fester in agony. Somehow, in the 20th century United States the same reasoning isn't followed for people. The first concern is always save the life, no matter what the cost in dollars or in subsequent loss of quality of life. In many cases, we extend the dying process, which might naturally take minutes or months, to years. In many cases families, which could go through a normal grieving process then get back to living their own lives, are dragged through a years-long process that can bankrupt them, both financially and emotionally.

"I came that you might have life and have it abundantly."

In nature, which God created, the weak, the sick, and the injured are quickly consumed by predators, allowing the strong of all species to survive. We are not animals, and we are not to live like animals; we are to protect our young, our sick, and our elderly, but God's way is that the strong survive to live full lives. The lives of the healthy should never be destroyed by the medical intervention in the lives of the diseased or injured. And the afflicted themselves should never have their agony prolonged. We must escape from the premise that death is an enemy to be avoided at all costs. Sometimes death is preferable to an alternative full of medical intervention, but devoid of *life*.

In the futuristic film *Bicentennial Man*, due to a manufacturing quirk, an android (played by Robin Williams) is produced who possesses creativity, intelligence, personality, what many of us would call a soul. His owner encourages his creativity and development and eventually grants him freedom. He seeks legal recognition as a "person" but is denied it because he is essentially immortal. He eventually falls in love with a human and as she ages, he realizes that he is destined to a life filled with continually losing everyone he cares about. Medical technology has improved to the point that his common law wife could have organs replaced and DNA repaired as needed to significantly extend her life, but she refuses, saying there is a natural order to things: We are born. We live. And when our time comes we die, and others take our places. William's character decides that this is a better way, and has his mechanical parts replaced with organs and body systems that will wear out so that he ages along with his wife and dies with her. He chooses to live well, love much, and laugh often rather than to live long.

On the other end of the life cycle is the question of what to do in the case of an unwanted pregnancy. Many Christians believe the only option is adoption. There are two interrelated problems with this "simple" solution. First, I ask how many of the women advocating this solution could give away the babies that they had been carrying in their wombs for nine months? I know I couldn't. The second issue is that to bring a healthy baby into the world requires some lifestyle changes that an expectant mother has great motivation to make; a woman with no intentions of raising this child does not have that motivation. To bring a healthy baby into the world requires adding healthy snacks to the diet, regular medical check-ups, refraining from alcohol, limiting use of over-the-counter medications, taking daily vitamins, limiting use of caffeine, quitting smoking, abstaining from illegal drugs. It also means enduring physical discomforts: morning sickness, fatigue, mood swings, loss of figure, swollen ankles, the inability to cut your own toenails, the possibility of hemorrhoids, varicose veins, etc. It also makes it hard to date. All of these and more are a small price to pay for a mother bringing her own child into her family, but an unmarried girl who doesn't plan to keep the baby has no incentive to make lifestyle changes or endure physical discomforts.

Some unexpected pregnancies result in the creation of a new family, or a beautiful addition to another family, but the result of eliminating abortion as an option would not be a flood of healthy white babies distributed to loving adoptive families. A result could be young girls without husbands, income, maturity, or family support deciding to "raise" their unexpected babies, and low-birth weight, alcohol-fetal syndrome, or drug-addicted babies and babies with preventable birth defects of all races put up for adoption. There are not enough loving adoptive families now for imperfect and minority babies. Most young girls without financial, educational, or emotional support are not capable of turning an unexpected baby into a productive member of society. We end up with children raising themselves, running away, joining gangs. Even if the girl is older and decides to marry the baby's father or has other family support to raise the child, there is a high probability that the marriage will not survive. If a girl abandons her education to raise an unexpected child, there is a cost to society. It's possible that at some point in her life, the girl will begin to blame the unexpected child for the way her life is turning out. This could lead to emotional or physical abuse or neglect of the child. We don't need more of these problems in society.

No one argues that abortion is a "good" or an easy solution. Life is full of situations with no good answers. In a perfect world an unwanted pregnancy would never occur. But would it be a better world if every unwanted pregnancy ended in the birth of a child? Opponents of abortion have many reasons for their position. Some believe that a human soul is created the moment an egg and sperm unite and that God begins knitting a body to go with it at that moment. Some people believe abortion violates the sixth commandment. In the early weeks of a pregnancy it is difficult to distinguish the species of an embryo. Some people are pro-life because they are against violence, but there is much less violence in the vacuuming out of a less-than-one-inch embryo than in the slaughtering of domestic animals for our consumption. An unexpected pregnancy disrupts the life of the mother and can disrupt the lives of other related people. It can result in an unwanted child with the potential to be abused before or after birth. Prevention of unwanted pregnancies is obviously the best solution. Adoption and marriage are beautiful options. But the health of the child and the circumstances into which a baby will be born have to be taken into consideration.

Emotional and spiritual quality of life must be given as much consideration as quantity of life.

The Role of the Church

In the 1950's a form of charismatic fundamentalism swept the United States. Through channels such as Billy Graham's crusades and Campus Crusade many people underwent emotional conversions where they accepted a package of beliefs in exchange for personal salvation of their souls. Totally left out of this exchange was any responsibility for the rest of society with the possible exception that they were to encourage others to undergo this same type of emotional conversion. This "evangelical aim of bringing individual souls into a personal relationship with Christ did nothing to fulfill the Christian mandate to take concerted action against the social injustices of poverty, exploitation, and racism that plagued modern industrial society."[40] Would Jesus have anything against prayer, Bible reading and study, fellowship and worship with other believers? No, not as a first step. But that "spiritual milk" is not the goal. It should lead to a life of action, *doing* the work that Jesus did.

In charismatic fundamentalism, salvation is based on the answer to the question, "Do you accept Jesus Christ as your Lord and Savior?" In response to this kind of thinking, Jesus told the parable of "The Two Sons". In that parable, the first son said he would not go work in his father's field, but later changed his mind and did. The second son *said* he would, but did not. The first son represents those who do not claim to be followers of God or of Christ, but do God's work. The second son represents those who claim to be Christians, but do not do God's work. Jesus asked, "Which of the two did what his father wanted?" The response came, "The first." Jesus was pointing out that what matters is doing the work, not what you claim.

In the introduction to this book, I mentioned that I was actively involved in a traditional mainstream Protestant church even though I questioned some of the official doctrine of the church. I call on those kinds of churches to examine their doctrine. If creeds such as the Apostles' Creed are not relevant to the ongoing life of the church, why periodically recite them in services? Why include them as part of the official doctrine of the church? Why should people have to say they believe them to join the church? Why include responses such as "Christ has died, Christ is risen, Christ will come again" if it has no bearing on who the church is and what it does? I am not advocating taking the religion out of church, leaving it as a social club. I am advocating honesty in what a person is joining when he joins a particular church. My personal belief is that the church should be a group of people who believe in God and desire to follow His will. The mission of the church should be to educate and nourish young members. It should be a center for prayer to discern God's will and a coordinating hub for the work of God's people in God's world. I am not saying that all churches should fit this mold. If there are churches that truly believe and act on their current official doctrine, then that fits their true mission and it should remain as it is. What we need to reform is the current classification of religions.

We currently have three religions that believe and follow one supreme God: Islam, Judaism, and Christianity. Christians are defined as those who believe the New Testament of the Bible. Jews are defined as a cultural ethnic group who follow the Old Testament but reject the New Testament. Muslims are those who believe the prophet Mohammed and the Qur'an. In the sixteenth century, Christians in Central Europe who rejected the orthodox dogma of the trinity acquired the name Unitarians, and in North America in1961, the Unitarians merged with the Universalists. So there was a church that accepted belief in God without worship of Christ, but over the years, prayer became meditation and God's will is not discussed directly. So, those who believe in God and Jesus but reject Paul's Christ are left without their own community. Perhaps people who believe that the oldest books of the New Testament and those least influenced by Pauline theology contain the keys to the kingdom could constitute a fourth major religion. Followers of a newly defined branch of religion could be called Jesusites, or God-Fearers, or just followers of The Way.

In the early years of the fifth century, Christianity was dominated by two schools or traditions based on two of the great church centers. Antioch saw Jesus as the model of what all humans could become. The Church at Antioch was renowned for its followers' care for the poor, establishment of hospitals, and involvement in what would today be called a Social Gospel. This arose from their belief that humanity was capable of great good because God was capable of working through us.[41] Perhaps followers of the "new" branch could be called Antiochans.

The Unitarian and many other "fringe" churches which claim belief in God but not Christ have been around for hundreds of years, but because they have been ostracized by the established church as heretical, they have remained on the fringe. Respectable people joined mainstream churches, which grew and multiplied. Only those who had the strength of their convictions and the willingness to travel to the small fringe churches, which are few and far between, joined those. Those churches have grown much more slowly, not because there's anything wrong with their beliefs, but because many people were unaware of them or afraid to be branded heretics for even looking into them. I seek respect for churches which believe in God and what Jesus preached. I challenge existing God and Jesus oriented churches to boldly reach out to their communities without fear of being called heretical, and I challenge existing churches to redefine what they really believe and stand for. Heresy is defined by human beings who have chosen to believe the message of Paul (another human being). Jesus didn't hesitate to speak out against the church of his day; those who believe that their message is closer to that of Jesus than the mainstream churches should not hesitate to boldly speak their message.

Earlier in this book, I confessed my love of Christian music. Christian music has become very popular, with many Christian radio stations all across the country. Many of these songs extol the God of the Old Testament. Many praise the ideals which Jesus praised. But there are also many which are Christian in the most Pauline sense of the word. The Unitarian Universalist Church has written new words for many of the traditional hymns. But in the merger with the Univeralists they have thrown the baby out with the bath water and most of the songs do not mention God. It would be a fairly easy task to sort through and pick out some hymns from a Christian hymnal and some from the Unitarian. I hope that some popular musicians and radio stations would also adopt the new format.

For years, I have had reservations about the cross as a symbol of Christianity, and especially as an item of jewelry. If Jesus had been executed in an electric chair or by guillotine, would we hang one of those around our necks? Rejecting the death of Jesus as the central tenet of Christianity makes the cross an even less appropriate symbol of faith. Praying hands or the Christian fish would be appropriate symbols of a life of faithfulness. Followers of Jesus need an identity that separates them from the followers of Paul. My desire is not to increase division; we have too many denominations now. My desire is to bring unity in the simplicity of following Jesus, not creeds.

Wholeness vs. Health Maintenance

The medical industry has convinced us that it is not for us to judge whether we are healthy or not. When mothers give birth to babies they are given a schedule of when to come back to a doctor for immunizations and "well-child" visits. With this pattern established, mothers are told to continue bringing their children back for "well-child" visits even when no immunizations are needed. In some states, there are legal requirements for children to see a doctor annually in order to attend public schools. All this creates an unhealthy reliance on doctors. With this mindset, mothers tend to run to the doctor for every sore throat or earache. There are times when a child has a serious infection and needs an antibiotic that *cures* the infection. But antibiotics are massively over-prescribed and incorrectly used by patients resulting in a lessening of the miraculous properties of these wonder drugs. Americans have come to view disease as something that happens *to* them and medicine as something that *is done to* them. They take no responsibility for their own health. If a doctor can't make them well he must not be a very good doctor. Patients become passive receptacles of whatever medicines and treatments their doctors subject them to.

Most visits to doctors result in no tangible benefits to the patients. Very often what they result in is a referral to a specialist who will prescribe tests, leave the patient to worry about the results of the tests, then either prescribe more tests, prescribe drugs that do little good or recommend surgery.

127

Many Americans are on chronic prescriptions that they will need (often in increasing doses) for the rest of their lives. This is not health. This is a trillion dollar-a-year industry thriving off the dependence of the American public.

Billions of dollars worth of unnecessary tests are performed to protect doctors against lawsuits.[42] These tests cause undue stress on the patients. Stress suppresses the immune system, and can cause gynecological problems, headaches, or heart disease. It's linked to chronic fatigue syndrome, binge eating disorder, and can speed HIV progression.[43] Research has found that up to 75 percent of doctor visits are for health problems that are complicated by stress and tension.[44] If there wasn't a problem before the tests, there may be after them.

Doctors have a name for everything. If a child can't sit still and listen at school it's Attention Deficit Disorder, and their solution is to give the child drugs every day. If a person is depressed, that's a clinical disorder and they have drugs for that. If a person is lethargic it is Chronic Fatigue Syndrome, but to my knowledge there is not yet a prescription for that. If the doctor can't name your complaint, you are sent to specialists and subjected to tests until they can name it and you are sent happily with a prescription to the pharmacy. None of these medications cure the patient. They treat the symptoms usually causing side effects that often need their own treatment.

Despite hundreds of years of research, medical researchers have developed no cure for two of the most common illnesses, colds and influenza. Over a lifetime, the average person is subjected to some 24,000 hours of coughing, throat pain, congestion, and headache from colds.[45] The medical establishment offers flu shots to prevent whatever strain of flu they guess will be prevalent that year. Millions of dollars worth of over-the-counter remedies are sold each year to try to fend off the symptoms of a cold or flu, often causing their own side-effects and making the patient feel just well enough to go to school or work to spread the germs so others can enjoy the misery of a cold or flu.

Medical research is based on Hippocratic medicine which dates from 400-200 BC. It "taught that diseases had natural causes and could therefore be studied and *possibly* cured according to the workings of nature. Under Hippocratic medicine, a well-trained physician could cure illness with knowledge gained from medical writings or from experience. Modern medicine is still based on this assumption."[46] Some illnesses such as scurvy, malaria, yellow fever, and typhoid have yielded to this brand of medicine. But not content to settle for these victories, Hippocratic medicine has tried unsuccessfully to take over the entire spectrum of human physical and psychological complaints. It is woefully inadequate for this task.

Thomas Sydenham (1624-1689) "believed that medicine must be learned through experience at the patient's bedside and that the practice of medicine should be based on observation rather than book learning or theory." "He came to believe that medical treatment was justified by results, not by physiological theory."[47]

Clinical trials strive to achieve the perfect "passive receptacle" status. When clinical trials of experimental drugs are conducted, results of the new drug are compared to the effects of a placebo to eliminate the "placebo effect" of the new drug. Since the 1970s "double blind" studies are conducted in which neither the patients or the administrators of the subject drug know if they are receiving/giving the real drug or a placebo. But human beings are not passive receptacles. In conditions such as major depression, anxiety disorder, and panic disorder up to fifty percent of patients receiving placebo treatment respond favorably. Perhaps a more effective study would divide the patients into two groups and tell one group they are receiving an experimental drug and the results are unknown. Tell the other group "Take these. You should feel fine in 7 days." Give both groups a placebo. I would wager that in most instances the difference in expectation would yield a more striking contrast in the results of the two groups than a difference in what is in the tablet. This would prove that pursuit of a pharmacological treatment of some conditions is less promising than other non-pharmacological means. According to Herbert Benson, M. D., "between 60 and 90 percent of visits to physicians are prompted by conditions that are related to stress and are poorly treated by drugs and surgery."

Dr. Dale Matthews of Georgetown University estimates that about 75% of studies of spirituality have confirmed health benefits. "If prayer were available in pill form, no pharmacy could stock enough of it." In studies at several medical centers, prayer and faith have been shown to speed recovery from depression, alcoholism, hip surgery, drug addiction, stroke, rheumatoid arthritis, heart attacks and bypass surgery.[48] None of these studies attempted to determine whether there is a God or if he intervenes in our daily lives. The fact is that prayer brings about increased quality of life, healing, and longevity.

The Power of Healing

Whether the healings of Jesus were miraculous or not, they were not limited to just him. His followers healed many as well. Healing was a primary activity of the followers of Jesus. When Jesus sent out the twelve disciples, his instructions to them were, "Heal the sick, raise the dead...Freely you have received, freely give."[a] When Jesus sent out the seventy-two followers his instructions were, "Heal the sick"[b]. After Jesus was crucified, crowds brought their sick to the apostles "and all of them were healed."[c] The apostle Peter raised Dorcas from the dead[d], and Paul raised a young man named Eutychus[e]. This healing ability was lost over the years. A few people have claimed and others still claim to be

---

[a] Matthew 10:8
[b] Luke 10:9
[c] Acts 5:16.
[d] Acts 9:40
[e] Acts 20:9-10

able to heal others. But it has been lost as a major component of the life of the faithful. Americans who claim to have faith in an omnipotent God display more faith in bottles of tablets. All unwellness is not created equal. There are injuries and illnesses that are cured by conventional medical treatment. There is a middle category of conditions that respond well to ongoing treatment, though often with side effects. And there is a third category of illnesses and conditions that are only marginally improved by conventional medical intervention, if at all.

In my search for truth about Jesus' preaching and teaching I looked to the oldest books of the New Testament, but they characterize the healings of Jesus as simply miraculous. The early church destroyed any writings which may have existed about how Jesus and his followers healed. Or perhaps it was never written because it was a secret teaching handed down from master to disciple. The ancient Asian healing practices of Qigong (China) and yoga (India) were not originally written down for this reason, but they have survived and have since been written down. Both Qigong and yoga initiate a healing process by a cleansing breath, by exhaling the diseased life force or breath (unclean breath). As the process continues, the vacuum created by exhaling the diseased life force is replaced by a healing life force or breath of life. One Qigong master believes that the feet must be thoroughly planted on the ground while the diseased life force is being flushed from the body, and the practitioner should imagine it being buried underground so that it does not reattach itself to anyone or anything else, perhaps such as a nearby herd of pigs.

In his book *The Healer Within*, Roger Jahnke points out that all healing is accomplished by the body, even when medicines or other interventions are used to promote this healing. "When you cut yourself, the wound heals automatically. When you have a sprain or bruise, it heals automatically. When you have a broken bone, the physician must set the bone correctly, but then nature heals it spontaneously." Physicians administer treatment, but nature provides the cure. Believers of the omnipotent God have the ultimate treatment available to them. At no cost. Force out the diseased breath. Draw in the healing power of God. God can initiate the healing that our bodies can complete. That doesn't mean that we have no responsibilities. We have the responsibility to adopt a positive attitude, that we are not helpless victims of whatever plagues us. We have the responsibility to adopt a positive lifestyle including good nutrition, exercise, rest, etc. Jahnke's book outlines other steps we can take to promote the self-healing abilities of our bodies.[49] Health is not something that can be administered to us. We must be willing to change ourselves from patients into students of health.

To most western followers of the Judeo-Christian traditions, meditation is an alien practice. In his book, Roger Jahnke says prayer is when you talk to God; meditation is when you listen to God. He says it is this time of listening that activates the healing resources that all of us have within us. He says the most effective prayer is the most general: Thy will be done. When you have a cold or any other illness or injury, don't spend your time begging the king to give you healing. The omniscient God does not need to be informed that you have a problem. Spend time listening to God, quieting your own thoughts and emotions, concentrating on faith and love, triggering a relaxation response and a positive physiological response throughout the body, particularly in the immune system.[50] And who knows what God will speak to you if only you'll quiet your heart and listen.

Jahnke's book contains an intriguing statement. "In some forms of ... Chi Kung [Qigong] from China and Yoga from India, the capacities to forgive and surrender are the most elevated forms of healing and are called soul healing. These systems propose that when the soul is healed, it automatically clears the mind, and this automatically heals the body."[51] If true, this would explain how Jesus healed the sick and those with unclean spirits. Jesus offered forgiveness, healing the soul, resulting in the healing of the body. Jahnke also says that the natural healing resource, which we all possess and is enhanced by practices such as prayer/meditation, is multiplied when people join in these practices together in a group. He says that as people gain understanding of the nature of "healing fields" they can cooperate to produce healing potential to benefit others.[52] Jesus recruited twelve men to study under him, pray with him, and work with him. After he was killed, the eleven disciples selected a replacement for Judas and stayed together to study, pray, and carry out their mission to preach and to heal. Jesus perfected a way to tap into the healing power of God and shared it with his disciples who practiced it until they were distracted by Paul's adulteration of Jesus' message and mission.

The English word disciple is derived from a Latin word meaning pupil or student. "Modern" schools of healing and those that have continued from antiquity, i.e., Christian Science, traditional Chinese medicine, Yoga, refer to their practitioners as students. I don't think this is a coincidence. There are techniques that can be taught and learned to promote the body's natural healing power, both in oneself and others. This was one aspect of what Jesus taught his disciples which was substantially lost within one generation.

There are eight components of yoga paraphrased here from Iyengar's book *Yoga*.

1. a code of ethical behavior to be observed
2. discipline, a desire to follow the path
3. the generation and distribution of energy
4. the expansion and extension of life force
5. The mind is set free from objects that the senses desire.
6. The controlled mind is made to intensify its attention on a single thought.
7. peace, freedom from attachment
8. Self-awareness is lost.[53]

Qigong is more simply classified in three components: control of the body through postures and movements, control of the mind through meditation, and control of the breath and life force. The qigong component of control of the body roughly corresponds to the yoga component of generating energy, which is also accomplished through postures. Control of the mind roughly corresponds to the final three components of yoga and is accomplished through meditation. Control of the breath and life force roughly corresponds to expansion and extension of life force. While the philosophy and results of qigong and yoga are very similar, the methods are not. The postures of qigong are in direct contrast to the postures of yoga. This suggests that it is not the specific postures that contribute to the end goals, but rather the practice of daily discipline over the body.

It is certain that Jesus followed a code of ethical behavior, had discipline, and had control over his mind as epitomized by peace and unity with God. It is easy to imagine that Jesus had control over his breath and life force as illustrated by the scene where he recognizes that power had gone out of him when the woman touched him in the crowd. However, there is only anecdotal evidence that Jesus had greater than normal control of his body. Though the instances are few, they are incredible: the forty day fast, walking on the water, the resurrection. His daily practice seemed to only consist of prayer (perhaps on his knees with his hands folded or sitting cross-legged with his hands on his legs), and walking. Perhaps a half-hour of prayer in a specific posture and a half-hour of walking or other similar mild exercise on a daily basis is enough to maintain control over the body, especially when combined with a disciplined diet rich in fruit, vegetables, and grain and low in meats as advocated in yoga and, anecdotally, as practiced by Jesus.

Biblical evidence suggests that Paul possessed the Christian power of healing, but what he did with it suggests that he succumbed to the third temptation of the devil. Faced with similar power and the same choices as Jesus, Paul chose to use his power to build earthly kingdoms. He seeded churches with genuine Christian love and empty pagan promises and strove to maintain control of his growing fiefdom and secure immortality for himself through the writing of letters. Perhaps without Paul, Christianity would have taken much longer to spread outside of the country of Judea, but perhaps it would have spread in a much purer form, complete with the power of healing that was such an integral part of The Way of Jesus.

The Original Covenant

From the dust of the ground

The original covenant between God and his people required them to be faithful to him and to obey his commands. 1 Samuel says, "To obey is better than sacrifice."[a] The Old Testament contains many other truths. I believe the books of Exodus through Malachi give the history, values, hopes and

---

[a] 15:22

dreams of the Hebrew people. I believe the stories in Genesis of Noah's flood through the end of the book record the history of God's people as it had been handed down to Moses through oral tradition, containing historical truth through the filter of what was important to people and what impacted them emotionally. I believe the stories of creation through Cain and Able record the relationships between God and his creations. I do not believe in the historical accuracy of those early chapters; I believe what Mortimer Adler calls the "poetic truth" of those stories. We need the Old Testament to understand who we are, where we came from, and what our God requires. God created the earth, atmosphere, seas, sun, moon, stars, fish, birds, animals, man and woman. Did he do it in six days? It doesn't matter. Chapter 1 of Genesis is a poem, written to help the Hebrew people remember, and more importantly to celebrate that God created us and our world. There is another account of creation in chapter 2. It differs in the order in which things were created and makes no mention of time frames. It is in this account that we read that "God formed the man from the dust of the ground and breathed into his nostrils the breath (spirit) of life." Man is made of the same elements as the rest of the earth, but his spirit is from God.

What are we to make of the story of Adam, Eve, and the tree of the knowledge of good and evil? It presents itself as an explanation of women's pain in childbirth and the need to work to eat and touches on other important themes, but as a coherent story, it makes little sense. It is usually presented as man choosing to disobey God and thereby falling from His grace. God had commanded Adam not to eat from the tree of the knowledge of good and evil, or he would die, as if it were poisonous. The serpent told Eve that if she ate of the fruit she would be like God knowing good and evil. After Adam and Eve ate the fruit God said, "Man has now become like one of us, knowing good and evil." So it seems that God lied and the serpent was right. God did not create pets (what else could you call bipeds without the knowledge of good and evil) who *chose* to trade their life as innocent pets to become creatures of higher reasoning. A creature without knowledge of good and evil, by definition, cannot *choose* anything more abstract than "this fruit looks riper than that one."

Human women give birth in pain in part because human babies have heads enlarged by the addition of a cerebral cortex – the center of higher reasoning. So there is a direct correlation between women's pain in childbirth and the knowledge of good and evil. There is no scientific way that the writers of the Old Testament could have known this in the 15th century BC. It had to have come from the inspiration of God.

A garden could easily support two people. But Adam and Eve were fruitful and multiplied. As the population grew, man's higher reasoning ability allowed him to develop agriculture to avoid the painful toil of moving on to hunt and gather. Man *chose* the painful toil of agriculture. It was this fruit of man's higher reasoning ability that has allowed the population of the earth to continue to grow ever since. This is the poetic truth the story conveys.

"...Until you return to the ground, since from it you were taken; for dust you are and to dust you will return." The elements of which man is formed must be recycled like all other elements of the earth. So God banished Adam from the garden. "He must not be allowed to reach out his hand and take also from the tree of life and eat, and live forever."[a] God did not create man to live forever. God did not want man to live forever. Several generations later the LORD said, "My Spirit (breath) will not remain in[b] man forever, for he is corrupt (mortal); his days will be a hundred and twenty years."[c] God formed man out of the elements of the ground and breathed his life into his creation. He never intended for man to live forever, but after several generations, he is sure he doesn't want man to live forever. At the end of our lives, we all must commit our spirits into the Father's hands.

Not Adam but Cain

If you do what is right, will you not be accepted? But if you do not do what is right, sin is crouching at your door; it desires to have you, but you must master it.

-- Genesis 4:7

This is the poetic truth of the story of Cain and Abel. Cain didn't master sin. He killed his brother out of jealousy.

---

[a] Genesis 3:22
[b] Or contend with
[c] Genesis 6:3

Two people could get along on earth, but add a third and a fourth and one out of the four will not be able to master sin. Sin didn't enter the world through Adam eating a fruit. Sin entered the world through Cain giving in to his jealousy and murdering his brother.

In the story of Noah we read that whoever kills a person, shall be killed by man; "for in the image of God has God made man." This is a clear requirement for capital punishment. Opponents of capital punishment often cite the sixth commandment as their reason. The proper translation of that commandment is "You shall not murder." The punishment for breaking that commandment is clearly spelled out in Exodus. "Anyone who strikes a man and kills him shall surely be put to death. However, if he does not do it intentionally…he is to flee to a place I will designate. But if a man schemes and kills another man deliberately, take him away from my altar and put him to death."[a] One of the reasons the punishment for manslaughter was exile was that this was a mobile society. Prison was not an option. The list of capital crimes continues. The crime of killing a person who was made in God's image is so heinous that God doesn't want the perpetrator polluting his world. There is no shortage of bodies on this planet. We have no obligation to attempt to re-form what the parents have not formed well enough to abide by the basic rules of society. "Train … a child in the way he should

---

[a] 21:12

go, and when he is old he will not depart from it." We have no obligation to provide food and shelter without toil for those who contribute nothing positive to our society. If those who break the basic rules of our society wish to continue to live in it, they must contribute their share of toil and learn to respect the rules by which the game of life is played.

The story of the tower of Babel provides an explanation of how man came to be scattered over the earth speaking different languages. But it tells us far more about nature of both God and humankind. People said, "Come, let us build ... a city, with a tower that reaches to the heavens, so that we may make a name for ourselves." The LORD said, "If as one people speaking the same language they have begun to do this, then nothing they plan to do will be impossible for them." This creature of God's was growing too big for his britches. So, the Bible tells us, God went down and confused their language so they could not understand each other. Thousands of years later, translators make communications between languages possible, but cultural differences still make agreements between many nations impossible. With the development of steel, the race to build a tower that reached to the heavens to make a name for ourselves resumed. And we have had other races to prove who could build a nuclear bomb, who could reach the moon. The arrogance of nations is beyond being confused by language. Between individuals there is the race to see who can accumulate the most "toys". At this point, it would probably take some cataclysmic event to bring humility to God's creatures and refocus priorities.

Covenant

From the Tower of Babel, we move on to God's Covenant with Abraham. This covenant of land was repeated several times in Genesis. The wording in each is slightly different, but basically the promise from God was "To your descendants I give this land, from the river of Egypt to the great river, the Euphrates."[a] In verse 16:15 Abraham's first descendant was born: Ishmael, father of Arab Muslims. The relationship of Ishmael to the covenant is directly addressed. God said of Ishmael, "I will surely bless him; I will make him fruitful and will greatly increase his numbers. He will be the father of twelve rulers, and I will make him into a great nation. But my covenant I will establish with Isaac, whom Sarah [your wife] will bear to you by this time next year."[b] At this point God is talking about the more specific covenant in verse 17:8 "The whole land of Canaan, where you are now an alien, I will give as an everlasting possession to you and your descendants after you; and I will be their God." So there appear to be two covenants: A large area of land promised to Abraham's descendants and a subset of that land promised to those descendants who would be born through Isaac. These covenants are not in conflict. This is not to say that other countries necessarily should recognize this covenant, which may appear ephemeral to them.

---

[a] 13:15, 15:7, 15:18, and 17:4
[b] Genesis 17:18-21

Let's take this a step further. I am no expert on Islam, but the descriptions I have read of Allah and the descriptions in the Bible of Jehovah, God of Abraham and Isaac are identical. "We believe in that which has been bestowed upon us, as well as that which has been bestowed upon you: for our God and your God is one and the same, and it is unto him that we [all] surrender ourselves." Qur'an 29:46. In her book *A History of God*, Karen Armstrong includes this quote from Ibn al-Arabi : "Do not attach yourself to any particular creed exclusively, so that you may disbelieve all the rest; otherwise you will lose much good, nay you will fail to recognize the real truth of the matter. God, the omnipresent and omnipotent, is not limited by any one creed."[54]   From what I have read, the holiness, the piety required of Jews and Muslims is the same with the exception of no work on the Sabbath for Jews. In her book, Karen Armstrong says the intolerance that many people condemn in Islam today springs from Muslims' intolerance of injustice, whether this is committed by their own or by the powerful Western countries. She also describes the origins of the Arab practice of tribal revenge. In a mobile society, finding the specific perpetrator of a crime was often impossible. For this purpose, any member of the offending tribe could pay the punishment. This basic system of justice worked 2000 years ago. Today it simply spirals in a barbaric game of tit for tat. This intolerance of injustice along with a very strong attachment to creed is what all the fighting in the mid east is about.

Abraham's son Ishmael appears again in the Bible when Abraham sent him away[a]. God again says he will make Ishmael into a great nation, and verse 20 says, "God was with the boy as he grew up." But if he was with those twelve rulers as they led their nations, he didn't teach the people new methods of justice.

In the Gospel according to John, Jesus says, "I have other sheep that are not of this sheep pen. I must bring them also. They too will listen to my voice, and there shall be one flock and one shepherd."[b] Six centuries later Muhammad preached in Saudi Arabia. He considered himself to be a prophet of God, and Islam (surrender to God) spread just like Christianity had, attracting dozens, hundreds, thousands, then millions of followers. The religions of the sons of Ishmael and the sons of Isaac are not in conflict. Had Christ returned to bring his sheep of another pen? If so, there is certainly not one flock and one shepherd. Politics intervened and not only do Jews, Christians, and Muslims not consider themselves to be one flock with one shepherd, through history they have tended to have an adversarial relationship, each considering the others to be infidels and a political threat and slaughtering each other by the thousands.

There is a parable from Boccaccio's *Decameron* that the sixteenth century Italian church administrator Menocchio told during his inquisition for heresy. There was once "a great

[a] Genesis 21:14-21
[b] 10:16

lord who had declared that his heir would be identified by a special ring, but had three identical rings made for his sons so that each would think he was the legitimate heir in possession of the true ring. 'Likewise,' he told the inquisitor, 'God the Father has various children whom he loves, such as Christians, Turks, and Jews, and to each of them he has given the will to live by his own law and we do not know which is the right one.'"[55]

Soon after its introduction, "Christians of the east and west were quick to define Islam as a Christian heresy... Accordingly, John of Damascus depicted Islam as a perversion of Christianity." In the ninth century, the Spanish Christian Eulogius attacked Islam as the ultimate heresy. He was the first Christian to recognize Islam as a separate religion.[56] Islam has much more in common with our Judeo-Christian beliefs than most people realize.

Throughout history God has revealed himself to people. When Judaism was mature it declared, "God has finished revealing himself. There will be no more prophecy." When Christianity was mature it declared, "God has finished revealing himself. There will be no more prophecy." On these self-proclamations, they rejected all later revelations as false. But religious proclamations do not prevent God from revealing himself to men. Throughout the centuries, there have been many religious writings, many inspired by God, but all written by thoroughly fallible people. The Old Testament contains much factual history, and much inspired prophecy. The New Testament contains factual history and inspired writing. That does not make them infallible in their entirety. There is no religion that has a monopoly on religious truth. I believe the Qur'an also contains inspired words of God.

I have heard a couple of Christian ministers say that the only way there will ever be peace in the Middle East is for all the countries involved to unite under Jesus Christ. In their religiocentrism, they don't realize how offensive this is to both Jews and Muslims who comprise the vast majority of the population of the Middle East. The only way there will ever be peace in the Middle East is to put aside such selfish views and unite under the one God who is worshipped by all three religions. The moral laws of Christianity, Judaism, and Islam also have much in common. Adherence to these moral laws would do much to bring peace to the middle east. Muslims believe that Jesus was a prophet of God, but to raise him to the status of deity beside God is the ultimate blasphemy to the strictly monotheistic Muslims.

The Qur'an speaks directly about Jesus: "We believe in Allah, and in what has been revealed to us and what was revealed to Abraham, Isma'il, Isaac, Jacob, and the tribes, and in the books given to Moses, Jesus, the prophets, from their Lord; we make no distinction between one and another among them."[a] And: "We sent Jesus the son of Mary, confirming the Law that had come before him. We sent him the Gospel: therein was guidance and light, and confirmation of the Law

---

[a] Surah 3:84.

that had come before him: a guidance and an admonition to those who fear Allah."[a] And: "O Jesus the son of Mary! Did you say to men, 'worship me and my mother as gods?' He will say: 'Never could I say what I had no right (to say). Never said I to them anything except what You commanded me to say, to wit, "Worship Allah, my Lord and your Lord.""[b]

In Genesis chapter 22 we have the decisive testing of Abraham. In the pagan religions with which Abraham was surrounded, human sacrifices were common. In this atmosphere, God called him to sacrifice his son. Abraham prepared to do as God commanded, but at the last moment, God stopped him saying in effect, I had to know that you were willing to sacrifice your son to me, but I do not desire human sacrifices; sacrifice a ram to me. He has never since called for a human sacrifice.

Ten Commandments

Many Christians are content to believe the "right" things and to attend and participate in church functions. They worship and live the rest of the week as "good" people, not breaking many commandments, although some would like to simplify and shorten that list. Most don't have a problem obeying "You shall not murder." As soon as you get past that, some people start to find gray areas. "You shall have no other

---

[a] Surah 5:46.
[b] Surah 5:116-117.

gods before me." I don't worship Vishnu or Shiva, so I must be OK on that one. It doesn't have anything to do with spending all my waking hours earning money does it?

You shall not make or worship idols. But praying to a statue of the Virgin Mary is a good thing, isn't it? Hey, come take a look at my new car! A thousand years before the time of Jesus, God's competition took the form of Baals and Asherah poles. Two thousand years after the time of Jesus it takes the forms of movie stars, rock stars, sports stars, luxury cars, big-screen TVs, and even spoiled kids. Worship is adoration, but more importantly it is where your focus is, what you reach toward, how you spend your time.

"You shall not misuse the name of the Lord your God." But "Oh my God" is just a saying; I don't mean anything by it. Exactly.

"Remember the Sabbath day by keeping it holy." That means for an hour or two on Sunday mornings, right?

"Honor your mother and your father." A worthy goal, but some parents weren't ideal parents. Maybe they're not ideal people. It doesn't still apply to them, does it?

"You shall not commit adultery." Is that one still on the books?

"You shall not steal." Does that include office supplies for home use? Does it apply to questionable tax deductions? Does it include suing McDonalds for burning me with their coffee or making me fat?

"You shall not give false testimony against your neighbor." That just means in court, right? And then if my

149

lawyer instructs me to tell a white lie, I'm just doing what I need to. And it certainly can't apply to business transactions.

"You shall not covet your neighbor's house. You shall not covet your neighbor's wife...or anything that belongs to your neighbor." But it's OK to want a pool or a car like the one they got, right? Our capitalistic economic system has refined advertising into the high art of evoking covetousness. A successful ad campaign is one that leaves people thinking they have to have the product advertised. Advertisers use any means to get people to desire what they do not currently have. In the early days of capitalism, entrepreneurs identified an unmet need and produced the needed product or service. All they had to do was let people know that their product or service was now available, and those who wanted or needed it, purchased it. Most Americans have all of their physical needs met using only a percentage of their income. Advertisers' job is to get them to part with the rest of their income or more by convincing them that their lives would be much better if they bought their product or service. If Americans were unswayed by advertising, it wouldn't exist, but advertisers are successful in inciting covetousness among the population.

Many Christians are very fond of the saying "Christians aren't perfect, just forgiven." Very fond. It's *so* much easier to say Jesus died for my sins than to try to follow any of those rules. Let's have a reality check. God won't care if I sleep with my neighbor's wife because a good man was executed 2000 years ago. And my neighbor won't mind, as long as he doesn't find out. I go to church most Sundays. I serve on a couple of committees. That's my get into heaven free card, right? Nobody really expects me to follow those 3500-year-old laws, do they? Besides, who's it hurting?

Let's check it out using all of the preceding examples:

How would your life change if you spent more time with your baby getting off the bus than you spend on the baby in the driveway (or whatever your "idol" is)? Count the time you spend doing things like washing it and the extra time you spend working to earn the money to pay for what you have compared to more basic transportation. Or what if you spent that time helping your neighbors or working with the community?

Could millions of people saying "Oh my God" and meaning nothing by it be a reason that more prayers are not answered? You know the story about the boy crying wolf.

As far as I know, the commandment about keeping the Sabbath is about balance. A minimum of fourteen percent of your week should be dedicated to your spiritual life. Perhaps 35 percent of your week is spent earning a living, and 20 percent is spent doing life maintenance things like showering, cooking, eating, commuting, and cleaning. Some faith traditions have found ways to count some of this time as spiritual nourishment such as Jewish regulations surrounding cooking, eating, and cleaning. Reserving 14 percent of your time for nurturing your higher nature and rising above the things of this world insures that you won't get bogged down in the muck of this world. It's an investment that many of us can't even imagine the benefits of.

Sleeping with your neighbor's wife could lead to both you and your neighbors getting divorced and all the kids growing up without fathers and raised by day care providers and exhausted mothers. That might be good for lawyers, but it's not good for anyone else. There might not be anyone to help with homework or ask about things that come up while hanging out with friends. The kids could end up getting pregnant, using drugs, stealing things, vandalizing, or just not caring about other people. Would all of those things happen? Probably not. Wouldn't it be bad enough if one of them did?

Your company makes less profit or charges higher prices because of all the "shrinkage" caused by employees who take home office supplies or other inventory. That impacts either the shareholders or the customers or both. If you don't pay as much tax as you should, the tax rate has to be increased for the government to bring in the same amount of revenue, so honest taxpayers end up paying more than their share. When a company like McDonalds gets sued and either they or their insurance companies have to pay large settlements, that again means lower profits for shareholders, higher prices for customers, or both. In civil trials, legal minutia holds more weight than common sense. We don't take any responsibility for our own actions. Some company or government agency should be held responsible for our health and safety. Lawsuits have also had a significant impact on everyday lives. For example, elementary school teachers can no longer use seesaws to illustrate the properties of levers because liability means these inexpensive, fun (and educational) pieces of playground equipment are no longer installed on playgrounds.

Our court system is completely unrelated to a search for truth or justice. Which side wins in a trial? The side with the more expensive legal team. Truth has nothing to do with it. It's all about winning and making money. There are always legal loopholes or you can play the sympathy of the jury just right... There is usually so much delay between a crime and the trial that memories have been totally replaced by scripts. It could have happened; something like that happened. People who can't afford good lawyers go to jail. If they didn't commit that crime they committed ten others and didn't get caught. It's an average system of justice. There is so much crime and wrongdoing that we catch ten percent of the perpetrators and punish them ten times what they deserve for the nine times they didn't get caught.

Keeping up with the Joneses causes their warped sense of priorities to spread. It's one of the factors that drives us to spend all of our time and energy earning money to spend on things. If all Americans made a serious commitment not to covet anything that belonged to their neighbors or any of the products advertised on TV or other media, the world would be a simpler, much more pleasant and less violent place. Most of the products and services would still be available for those who wanted them, but they wouldn't pervade our lives as they do now, and they would be less expensive, because now a significant portion of corporate budgets is spent on advertising trying to convince people that they need or really want something they don't. People might be healthier, buying food and drinks that their bodies really crave instead of those advertisers have convinced people that they want.

"Now what I am commanding you today is not too difficult for you or beyond your reach...the word is very near you; it is in your mouth and in your heart so you may obey it. See, I set before you today life and prosperity, death and destruction. For I command you today to love the Lord your God, to walk in his ways, and to keep his commands, decrees and laws; then you will live and increase, and the Lord your God will bless you."[a] It was true in the time of Moses and it is true today.

Taking Stock: Where do we stand?

> *In the last century "the study of history was dominated by a new myth: that of Progress. It achieved great things, but now...we are, perhaps, beginning to grasp that it is as fictitious as most of the other mythologies that have inspired humanity over the centuries."*[57]
>
> *-- Karen Armstrong*

This applies both to our individual lives and our societies. General Omar Bradley said, "Ours is a world of

---

[a] Deuteronomy 30:11

nuclear giants and ethical infants. We know more about war than we know about peace, more about killing than we know about living." Throughout history, the educated have learned how to think and what the ramifications of thinking are. A classical, liberal education meant a thorough grounding in philosophy. In the past century and especially in the last generation there has been much specialization and a career orientation to education. People graduate from institutions of higher learning knowing how to build a nuclear bomb but having only had one course in history and one in ethics. There is an unhealthy compartmentalization of our lives. We get an education to get a job. Once we get a job, we do the job, usually without much thought about its impact on the world. We leave the "should we" questions for those higher up the ladder. At 5:00 (or whatever time) we leave the job behind and go on to live our lives as good people. This is true in medicine, in law, in engineering, and other disciplines. If we know how to do something, we do it without much thought as to whether we should. We often leave those decisions to the one paying the bill.

Universities are driven by the same thing that drives most institutions in the United States: the bottom line. Universities take in thousands of students and prepare them for a career. They supply courses for which there is a demand. Students get their "general education requirements" out of the way during their freshman year, so they can focus on their majors for the rest of their college careers. Many students major in dating and drinking or sports and search out the

155

easiest classes that will get them a BS or BA on their resume because employers look for degrees whether or not the requirements of the job demand knowledge gained from that education. Many of the great minds of the past were self-taught or developed under the auspices of a mentor. Companies and institutions requiring degrees or certifications instead of looking at the person's abilities and skills have caused many people who don't need and really don't benefit from a higher education to seek a degree. Many of the great inventions that have brought us to this point in history were invented by well-rounded individuals with a wide range of expertise. The modern specialization of knowledge has turned some of the most capable minds in the country into cogs on a wheel and deteriorated their quality of life. Corporations "own" the inventions of their employees.

Every day people struggle to "get ahead". Get ahead of what? What is it that people hope to gain in this struggle for more? In the United States, most people don't struggle for food, shelter, or basic clothing, or if they do it's after they have already paid the cable bill. They may struggle to get, or because they already have, a bigger house. They may struggle to buy the latest in designer clothing. It seems to be wired into the American consciousness that the key to happiness is more income to buy more things. So hourly workers work more hours to bring home a bigger paycheck. Mothers and fathers both work to bring in more income. Salaried employees work longer hours in hopes of getting a raise or promotion. All of them spend more time away from home, family, friends, and community. They don't invest time in building relationships because all their time is invested in earning money.

Fewer people are getting married in the first place, and 50 percent of those who do end up getting divorced. If you ask people what is important to them, the top four responses are good health, high integrity, good marriage, and good friends.[58] If you only surveyed people with children living at home, family would probably come out pretty high on the list. But if you ask people how they demonstrate that marriage, family and to a smaller extent friends, are important to them, I bet you would get a lot of answers that involve spending money on them, and very few that involve spending time with them. When our actions are in conflict with our values we experience stress. When our actions are in tune with our values we experience power.[59]

In a 2005 survey, college freshmen were asked to indicate which personal goals they consider essential or very important. Seventy-five percent picked "Being very well off financially".[60] Compare this percentage to those students who gave high ratings to several life goals or objectives in 1994 and 1976:

High school seniors extremely important personal goals		
	1994	1976
Having a good marriage & family life	76 %	75 %
Being successful at work	63 %	53 %
Having lots of money	26 %	15 %
Making a contribution to society	24 %	18 %

With the passage of 18 years there was a 19 percent increase in the number of students rating being successful at work as extremely important and a 73 percent increase in the number of students rating having lots of money as extremely important. There was also a 33 percent increase in the number of students rating making a contribution to society as extremely important. No definition of being successful at work was given, so presumably it includes both intangible factors such as satisfaction and tangible factors such as promotions. Seventy-five percent of 18-year-olds have a life goal of being very well off financially. Why? They obviously believe that money can buy happiness. Twenty years further into their lives that belief wears thin, but in their most creative years, the years which determine their life direction, this is what is driving them.

According to Rabbi Harold Kushner in *Who Needs God,* "the celebration of the man-made become[s] boring precisely because it cannot lift us beyond ourselves." Americans of the 21st century are obsessed with celebrating (and decorating and shopping for) holidays. The year starts slowly (on a hangover from all the festivities at the end of the year) with not much happening until Valentine's Day. Valentine's Day is not a major holiday, but it is not a private holiday just for couples. There are all sorts of candy, cards, jewelry, and trinkets to buy. School children exchange massive quantities of candy and cards. This is enough to hold most people till Easter, or at least till Mardi Gras which has been growing in popularity every year for the past decade. For many Americans, the only religious significance to Easter is the need to buy a new outfit (complete with hat and purse) for their semi-annual pilgrimage to church. The holiday is dominated by the Easter bunny, baskets of candy, decorated eggs, and a nice brunch or dinner. This sustains most people until the 4th of July, an inoffensive holiday dominated by cookouts and fireworks.

There is then a lull in major holidays to allow people to gear up for the back-to-back holidays of Halloween, Thanksgiving, Christmas, and New Year's Eve. Halloween, like the up-and-coming Mardi Gras, is much more popular than the associated Christian holiday, All Saints Day. It gives people a chance to revel in the dark underside of the spiritual world and gives kids a chance to dress up and solicit massive quantities of candy. This lasts until it is time to decorate for Thanksgiving which has become much more about food than thanks. If you wait until Thanksgiving is over to start preparing for Christmas you are way behind the curve. You can't possibly do all the shopping, wrapping, decorating, shipping, baking, partying, traveling, and card-writing you are expected to do if you wait that long. And, oh yes, you'll have to pick up a new outfit for the Christmas Eve service at church. Then it's on to New Year's Eve to drink, eat, and dress up. If you have kids, scattered among the rest of the holidays you have birthday parties to throw and endless birthday gifts to buy and wrap for the parties your kids are invited to.

I believe the dominance of holidays is due to the lack of meaning in the rest of people's lives. Life is dull if there's not a holiday to prepare for or celebrate. The celebration of these holidays has little to do with their "original" significance. Easter, which should be the biggest holiday for those who believe in the resurrection of Christ, is a relatively minor holiday. Many employees don't get any time off work for Easter, which always falls on a weekend. If kids get time off from school, they get "spring break" which encourages families to take a secular vacation at this time. If the holiday had a better mascot it would probably be celebrated in a bigger way, but the flimsiness of the Easter bunny hasn't stopped people from decorating and buying gifts. The celebration of a mid-winter festival predates the birth of Jesus. Christians usurped the pagan holiday in the fourth century AD, but the pagan elements of feasting, gift-giving, and decorating still dominate Christmas. It would be much more honest to call the holiday a mid-winter festival rather than *Mass* of *Christ*, which many don't celebrate and some don't even believe in. Why should Jewish people, Muslims, and other religious groups be left out of decorating and other festivities that have nothing to do with Jesus? Why should followers of Jesus feel like they have to decorate, exchange gifts, and send cards if they would rather remember Jesus by living the way he advocated?

One way to avoid the commercialism and excess of American holidays is to celebrate different holidays. Martha Zimmerman advocates this in her book *Celebrate the Feasts of the Old Testament in Your own Home*. Actually, she is probably advocating celebrating the Jewish feasts *in addition to* Christian holidays, but in order to celebrate both, you would have to simplify your celebration of Christian holidays.

Included in her observance of feasts is the Jewish Sabbath. In combining the Jewish and Christian observances she seems to advocate observing Sabbath from sundown Friday until Monday morning. A more realistic combination for most of us would be from sundown Saturday evening until Monday morning. By celebrating feasts in ways that are similar to the way they were celebrated 3000 years ago, it is impossible to get caught up in modern commercialism.

Where to from here?

One explanation I've read for why Christianity evolved from what it was in the first century AD to what it is now was to appeal to the masses. "The majority of 'self-professed Christians' were incapable of living up to the standard of the true church, which consisted of the "community of those who live in holiness."" This quote is attributed to Hippolytus in *The New Birth of Christianity*. Jesus did not preach to an elite; he preached to the rabble. He clearly thought that the masses were *capable* of following him, although he did not expect that the majority *would* follow him. It is a matter of choice. Anyone *can* live a right life. The question is "Who will?"

Americans today live with an explicit "What's in it for me?" philosophy, but all people need some sort of incentive to do anything. Why should anyone follow the way that Jesus set out? In the book of John, Jesus said those who didn't love him wouldn't obey his teaching.[a] If everyone followed it, the world would be a much better place, but the fact is that there will never be a time when everyone does what is right. The benefits of giving in to temptations are usually immediate, but the price is paid later. Many people are not willing to bypass the immediate benefits of doing what is destructive in the long run. Traditionally, the benefits of Christianity were billed as being in the "hereafter". The real benefits of living a good life are in the here-and-now: love, joy, peace; patience, kindness, goodness, faithfulness, gentleness and self-control.[b] Are you willing to change the way you live your life to bring love, joy, and peace into your life?

> *"In all probability, disappearance of piety toward the gods will entail the disappearance of loyalty and social union among men as well, and of justice itself, the queen of all the virtues."*
>
> -- Celsus from
> *The Four Witnesses*

This is what is wrong with the United States in the 21st century. Throughout history, religion has been an important shaping factor in who people were and what they did. This nation founded on freedom *of* religion has embraced the ideal of freedom *from* religion. People fled to the United States

---

[a] 14:24
[b] Galatians 5:22.

because the countries they came from did not allow them to worship as they believed they should. It is embodied in our constitution that there will never be a state-sponsored religion. Most importantly, this should mean that everyone is allowed to worship the way they believe they should. It also means that tax dollars will never be spent to teach people to follow one particular religion. It should mean that if someone believes they should pray in a certain way at a certain time and they happen to be on government property at that time, that they are allowed to do it. It should never mean that no one is allowed to practice any religion on government property be it local, state, or federal. That is what communist countries tried to do.

Religion has always been the incentive for moral behavior. Now we have a generation rejecting religion. The poor and uneducated have turned to alcohol, drugs, and violence; those with means have turned to adultery, embezzlement, and apathy. There is a small group that maintains high moral standards without practicing religion, but most of these were raised with religion as children.

We can only ask, where will the generations to come receive their moral education? The traditional source of religious education has been rejected by many. Almost no instruction of any sort takes place in most "homes" today. "Home" for many is simply a place to go when not at work, school, or all of the other places people would rather be. It is a place to grab some food, some sleep, with people that they know and possibly care about. It's the place where the TV is, the computer is, the electronic games are. There has been talk of the "cocooning" of America: people withdrawing from society within their four walls. Cocooning sounds cozy: Families banding together to be reborn as something new and better. That's not what's happening. If there are four people in the family they are often in four different rooms, possibly looking at four different electronic screens or in one room staring at one screen. People don't know their neighbors any more. People aren't in bowling leagues or bridge clubs. There are lots of activities revolving around children, but adult participation in these is usually limited to chauffeuring. Cocooning isn't cozy; it's destroying the fabric of society. People have no attachments to other members of society. They have become totally self-centered. Incidents of road rage demonstrate the total lack of connection people feel toward others in the same situation. There are only three ways to prevent the complete moral decay of our country: reform the entertainment industry so that TV, movies, and video games raise instead of lower the moral standards of America, add moral education to the public school system along with reading, writing, and arithmetic, or God would need to reach out in a new way to a populace largely unaffected by the current religious systems in place.

Entertainment reform will not happen because we are a nation that values two things – freedom of speech and capitalism. Freedom of speech has been interpreted to mean capitalists have the right to broadcast whatever people will pay for, either directly or indirectly. People pay to see what is exciting, funny, intriguing. They won't pay for (except on rare occasions) what is morally uplifting. We could trust God to reach out to people in a new way that affects how people live. Or we could be the hands through which God reaches out. When I lived in Florida, I was a volunteer teacher for "Learning for Life." Learning for Life helps youth in kindergarten through 12th grade develop social and life skills, assists in character development, and helps them formulate positive personal values. Resources and support for this program are available nationwide. (www.learningforlife.org). I assume the school had volunteers administer this program so it would not be an additional burden for teachers. In one hour a week (more or less – the program is flexible) through fun activities, the kids learned things that many of them would not be exposed to through any other source. Since the program was taught by volunteers, it also provided the opportunity for the kids to develop a trusting relationship with another adult besides (hopefully) their regular teacher and parents. If none of these things happen we can sit back and watch the country crumble for lack of a moral spine.

Outside these walls

W hy do people hide within their four walls when they're not at work or school? The United States has become an extremely mobile society. National and international companies mean that employees can be transferred to another state. Easy communication through the internet makes it easier than ever to get a job in another state. The instability of the economy makes it more likely than ever that people have to change jobs, which often means moving to a new community. It used to be that moving to a new community was the exception rather than the rule, so the rest of the community would break out the "welcome wagon" to welcome the newcomers and integrate them into the community. Now society has become so transient that the established community is not sufficient to welcome and incorporate all the newcomers. There is an attitude of "Why bother, they'll just move on in a few years", or "We don't even know the last people who moved in" or "We're still newcomers ourselves". On the part of those moving in there may be an attitude of "Why get involved, we'll just be moving on in a few years." There is no sense of belonging, no sense of home on the outside of these four walls. It's relatively safe and familiar inside.

Some Christians feel called to missionary work in far away lands, as if there were none here in the United States who need to hear the word of God. Within the United States those who feel called to go into missions work usually travel to another state, as if there are none within their own state who need to hear the word of God. Many thousands of dollars are spent on travel that could be put to better use closer to home. Jesus found plenty to minister to within walking and boating distance of his hometown. I think that many undertake missionary journeys either because of a touristic desire to visit a particular region or out of an arrogant "Our religion is better than your religion" attitude.

I don't know how many people are actually converted to Christianity by traveling missionaries, but of those who are, many were probably good people who practiced other religions before their conversion. Were these lost sheep that needed to be found or good sheep happily belonging to another flock? Most missionaries perform noble service for the people they minister to, and I do not mean to belittle the services that they perform. I just think they could be more efficiently and effectively performed by training and financing people who live closer to the needs. I bet many missionaries actually achieve none of their stated purpose to win converts for Christ, but serve other stated and unstated objectives both for the communities they serve and the churches that support them. There is a movement called indigenous missions. In one case, a man returned to his own people in his own country after training and started 100 churches. In another case, a man returned to his own people and had 225,000 students in a traveling Bible study. This is much more effective than sending someone who has to learn the language and the culture and will always be an outsider.

"How many more souls are to pass into eternity without having heard the name of Jesus?" This quote is attributed to a missionary a century ago. The answer is that it doesn't matter if they've heard the name; what matters is how they are living. Jesus said, "Why do you look at the speck of sawdust in your brother's eye and pay no attention to the plank in your own eye?" Why do you condemn others (or find them in dire need of "salvation") for not *believing* what you believe, and pay no attention to the way you are *living* your life? Jesus was not condemning the masses for sinning in the sense of breaking commandments; he was condemning them for not loving their neighbors enough. The spirit of God, the word of truth does need to be spread, but it needs to start within your own heart and be spread to the people in your family and your neighborhood and the people within a 50-mile radius of where you live and work. To realize the benefits of the kingdom of God on earth we need to work within our own communities. There are foreign communities that can have an impact on how we live our lives, but they are not open to the work of missionaries. If we start at home with the way we spend our time, attention, and money we can transform our country into the Kingdom of God.

Practically speaking, how do we transform our corner of the world? If you don't know your neighbors, you could start by getting to know them. Invite them to dinner, to play cards, or whatever you find non-threatening. Why should you get to know your neighbors? Because the first step to caring about someone is to know them, and caring enough to act is how we transform the world. You say you don't have the time. Everyone has 168 hours in every week; if you sleep 8 hours a night, you have 112 waking hours a week. If you work 40 hours, you still have 72 hours. Are you spending it parked in front of the TV or computer? Are you spending 60 hours a week working and commuting? If so, why? Don't just accept the way your life currently is. As the song says, you must learn to "look at life through heaven's eyes." Once you have evaluated what you are currently doing with your time, you must cut back on the time that is not contributing to making your life heaven on earth. You may be able to do this just by making a personal decision or it may involve talking to a boss or volunteer director or anyone else that has come to expect the way you are currently spending your time.

Once you take control of your time, you need to decide how to match your gifts to the needs in your community. Will you work with underprivileged children? The elderly? The homeless? Those in prison? Will you organize efforts for those groups to minister to each other? There are many successful programs that match nursing home residents without many loved ones to children or prisoners who don't have many who care about them. Through writing letters, drawing pictures, and other interactions the elderly gain new meaning for their lives and the children or prisoners get someone who cares about them and can share invaluable lessons about life.

Caring about people and having people who care about us is what makes life worth living. It doesn't have anything to do with what you wear or what you drive or where you live. The way of abundant life is to reach out to others in love, to live in a way that harms none and to forgive anyone who may have harmed us. It is to cultivate health within our selves through spending time with the Spirit and to share that vitality with others. What price are you willing to pay for good health, high integrity, good marriage, and good friends? Are you willing to change the way you live?

We need to break free from the delusion that believing what a missionary taught 2000 years ago will earn us an eternity surrounded by people with wings and harps. Life is now. You may have one year; you may have ninety. If you like harp music go to a concert. If you want love, joy, and peace, live the way that Jesus taught.

Hear, O Israel, the Lord our God, the Lord is one. Love the Lord our God with all your heart and with all your soul and with all your mind and with all your strength. Love your neighbor as yourself. There is no commandment greater than these.

Outside these walls

Notes

[1] http://www.religioustolerance.org/chr_poll7.htm#spir
[2] Carrier, Richard, "The Formation of the New Testament
        Cannon", http://www.infidels.org/library/modern/
        richard_carrier/NTcanon.html
[3] Chidester, David, Christianity – A Global History, (Harper
        SanFrancisco, 2000), p. 520.
[4] Ibid., p. 553.
[5] Frazer, James, *The Golden Bough*, (New York: Oxford
        University Press, 1994)
[6] Romer, John, *Testament – The Bible and History*, (Henry
        Holt and Company, New York, 1988), p. 338.
[7] Palmer, Martin, *The Jesus Sutras*, Ballantine Publishing
        Group, 2001), p. 88.
[8] "Early Christian History", B.A. Robinson, (Ontario
        Consultants on Religious Tolerance, 2003)
[9] Elliott, William J., *A Place at the Table*, (Doubleday, New
        York, 2003), p. 234
[10] Ibid., p. 201.
[11] Ibid., p. 205.
[12] Ibid., p. 362.
[13] Ibid., p. 229.
[14] Palmer, Martin, *The Jesus Sutras*, (Ballantine Publishing
        Group, New York, 2001), p. 94.
[15] Armstrong, Karen, *A History of God*, (Alfred A. Knopf, Inc.,
        1993), p. 280.
[16] Chidester, David, *Christianity – A Global History*, (Harper
        SanFrancisco, 2000), p. 349.
[17] Ibid., p. 351.
[18] Chidester, David, *Christianity – A Global History*, (Harper
        SanFrancisco, 2000), pp. 28-43.

[19] Armstrong, Karen, *A History of God*, (Alfred A. Knopf, Inc., 1993), p. 228.

[20] Elliott, William J., *A Place at t he Table*, (Doubleday, 2003), p. 230.

[21] Kushner, Harold, *To Life! A Celebration of Jewish Being*, (Little, Brown and Co. 1993), p. 289.

[22] Mitchell, Stephen, *The Gospel According to Jesus*, (Harper Collins Publishers, 1991), p. 87.

[23] Ibid., p. 41.

[24] Leavenworth, E.C.S., "The Essenes and the Dead Sea Scrolls at Qumran", http://Members.aol.com/wisdomway/deadseascrolls.htm

[25] Manitara, Olivier, "The Teachings of Jesus the Essene", www.essenespirit.com/jesus.html

[26] "Essenes", http://www.themystica.com/mystica/articles/e/essenes.html

[27] Crossan, John Dominic, *The Birth of Christianity*, (Harper SanFrancisco, 1999), p. 263.

[28] http://www.census.gov/prod/3/97pubs/cb-9701.pdf

[29] www.futureofincome.org/information2846/information_show.htm?doc_id=83485

[30] www.ncpa.org/~ncpa/pd/economy/ecob2.html

[31] www.ncpa.org/~ncpa/pd/economy/ecob2.html

[32] http://www.census.gov/prod/3/97pubs/cb-9701.pdf

[33] Chidester, David, *Christianity – A Global History*, (Harper SanFrancisco, 2000), p. 509.

[34] Kushner, Harold, *To Life! A Celebration of Jewish Being*, (Little, Brown and Co., 1993), p. 159, 189

[35] Hooker, Richard, "The Hebrews After the Exile", www.wsu.edu, 1996

[36] Chidester, David, *Christianity – A Global History*, (Harper SanFrancisco, 2000), p. 57.

[37] http://www.corporations.org/system/top100.html

[38] Barrigan, Daniel, *The Raft is not the Shore*," 1975.

[39] Chidester, David, *Christianity – A Global History*, (Harper SanFrancisco, 2000), p. 85.
[40] Ibid., p. 522.
[41] Palmer, Martin, *The Jesus Sutras*, (Ballantine Publishing Group, 2001), p. 94.
[42] http://www.aahpechochamber.tv/malpractice/number.htm
[43] http://www.stress.about.com/cs/medicalconditions/
[44] Jahnke, Roger, *The Healer Within*, (HarperSanFrancisco, 1999), p.93.
[45] http://www.theatlantic.com/issues/2000/10/fisher.htm
[46] Scarborough, John, Ph.D., "Hippocrates", World Book Multimedia Encyclopedia, 1999.
[47] Ramesy, Matthew, Ph.D., "Sydenham, Thomas", World Book Multimedia Encyclopedia, 1999.
[48] Hales, Dianne, "Why Prayer Could Be Good Medicine", *Parade Magazine*, March 23, 2003.
[49] Jahnke, Roger, *The Healer Within*, (HarperSanFrancisco, 1999), p. 8.
[50] Jahnke, Roger, *The Healer Within*, (HarperSanFrancisco, 1997), p. 101.
[51] Ibid., p. 181.
[52] Ibid., p. 223.
[53] Iyengar, BKS, *Yoga* (Dorling Kindersley, Ltd., 2001), p. 29.
[54] R.A. Nicholson, ed., *Eastern Poetry and Prose* (Cambridge, 1922), p. 148.
[55] Chidester, David, *Christianity – A Global History*, (Harper SanFrancisco, 2000), p. 349.
[56] Ibid., p. 175.
[57] Armstrong, Karen, *A History of God*, (Alfred A. Knopf, Inc., 1993), p. 295.
[58] http://www.afajournal.org/cover/family_1asp
[59] Smith, Hyrum, *What Matters Most*, (Simon & Schuster, 2000), p. 65.
[60] http://www.bpnews.net/bpnews.asp?ID=24784

NOTES

www.ingramcontent.com/pod-product-compliance
Lightning Source LLC
Chambersburg PA
CBHW021231090426
42740CB00006B/479